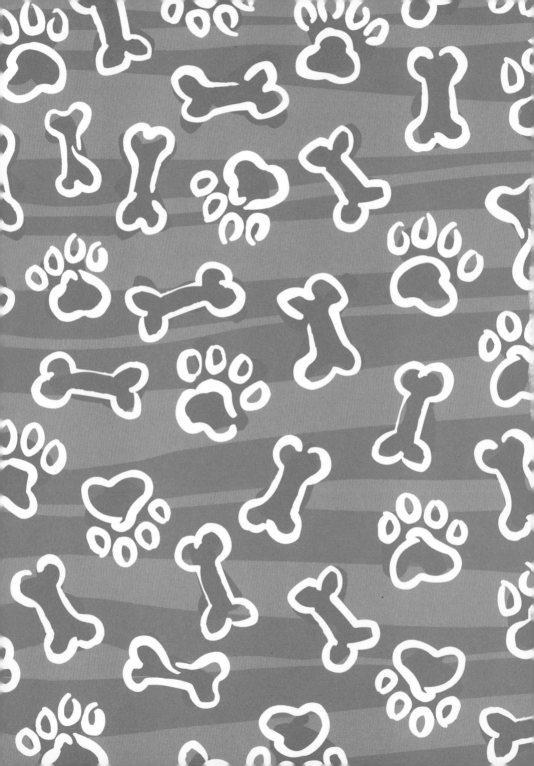

These Happy Tails are for

_____

May these stories inspire you
to a deeper love of dogs
and their Magnificent Creator.

Published in Nashville, Tennessee, by Thomas Nelson, Inc.®

Unless otherwise noted, Scripture quotations are taken from the *Holy Bible,* New King James Version. Copyright © 1979, 1980, 1982, Thomas Nelson, Inc.

Scripture quotations marked NIV are taken from the *Holy Bible,* New International Version® copyright © 1973, 1978, 1984, by International Bible Society. Used by permission of Zondervan Publishing House. All rights reserved.

Scripture quotations marked NLT are taken from the *Holy Bible,* New Living Translation, copyright © 2002. Used by permission of Tyndale House Publishers, Inc., Wheaton, Illinois 60189. All rights reserved.

Project Editor: Jessica Inman
Project Manager: Lisa Stilwell

Designed by: Greg Jackson, ThinkPen Design

ISBN-10: 1–4041–0527–1
ISBN-13: 978–1–4041–0527–0

Printed and bound in China
www.thomasnelson.com

happy tails

inspirational stories for dog's best friend

linda hultin winn

THOMAS NELSON
Since 1798

NASHVILLE   DALLAS   MEXICO CITY   RIO DE JANEIRO   BEIJING

Table of Contents

Introduction

Have you ever noticed that a dog's tail is his Geiger counter of happiness? It radiates the joy in his heart as his master approaches. Your dog probably knows the joy of your presence, too. And when you reach down to caress his sweet face, your simple touch causes him to prance, dance, and sing your praises.

Do you also know the joy of being in the presence of your Master—Almighty God, the Lord of all creation? He is the one who provides all your needs; keeps you safe through the storms of life; forgives you in spite of all the things you've done wrong; loves you even more than you love your dog; and wants to adopt you into His family. It is my hope that you'll meet Him in the pages of this book.

At the heart of *Happy Tails* you'll read a story of rescue and restoration as the loving adoptions of Mac and Bo parallel the testimony of all believers who have been adopted into God's family and the permanent, loving home He has prepared for us.

Happy Tails is divided into three sections:

"Rescued by the Good Master" introduces you to the work of canine rescue groups and Mac and Bo, two English Springer Spaniels adopted by my husband and me after they landed in a rescue program.

Through the life events of Mac and Bo, "Life with the Good Master" illustrates how much God loves us and wants us near Him on good days and bad. Bo would tell you, "Happy is the dog whose tail wags for the Good Master for he shall walk in freedom." Mac would be more apt to say, "Happy is the dog whose tail wags for the Good Master for he shall be forgiven."

In the last section, "In Search of the Good Master" offers expert insight into the heart of rescue dogs; Web sites that lead good masters to good dogs available for adoption; and man's road to rescue and adoption into God's family.

As you read *Happy Tails* you'll enjoy recalling similar dog tales from your own experience; discover practical solutions to doggy dilemmas like getting "skunked;" and in a quiet moment when your dog rests his head on your lap, you might even take a moment to rest your head in the everlasting arms of your Good Master.

Sprinkled throughout you'll find Scripture verses from God's Word; training tips from foster mom and obedience instructor, Christi Cooper; quips, quotes, and sage advice; suggestions for items to fetch for your dog; and other anecdotes.

It is my hope that as you read this book you will not only be encouraged to adopt your next dog but to ask God to adopt you into His family. For the dog who finds a permanent, loving home with the Good Master wags a happy tail.

*He brought me out
into a spacious place;
he rescued me because
he delighted in me.*

PSALM 18:19 NIV

RESCUED BY THE GOOD MASTER

Rescue Groups:

"Good Samaritans" of the Dog World

'Take care of him; and whatever
more you spend, when I come again,
I will repay you.'

LUKE 10:35

Every dog in a rescue program is there because people care enough to offer it hope, help, and healing. They choose to exercise their God-given dominion over animals by coming to their rescue and loving them.

As in the parable of the good Samaritan, these generous benefactors come alongside dogs who have been beaten, abandoned, or broken in spirit to restore them to good health, pick up the tab, and find them good homes. My dogs, Mac and Bo, both benefited from such care, but Mac's expenses exceeded the routine physical with heartworm check, vaccinations, and neutering. His hip repair totaled $1,700.

Nobody knows why Mac ran loose on a busy Atlanta street. He had no collar or ID chip to help locate his owner when he fell victim to a hit-and-run driver and lay helplessly on the side of the street. Although many people must have witnessed the accident, they passed by, not wanting to get involved. Only one compassionate woman stopped to lend a helping hand. In her great mercy, she picked him up, put him in her car, drove him to her vet, then contacted English Springer Spaniel Rescue. Thus began Mac's journey to restored health and a new home.

Bo's case was different. As a puppy, Bo was a Christmas present to a family who loved him and let him live inside with them. When he grew to fifty pounds at six months of age, Bo was tied to a tree in the backyard with only a shed to crawl under for shelter. There he cried for five years for his family to love him again. When his owner decided he didn't want Bo to spend another harsh winter out in the cold, he called English Springer Spaniel Rescue to come get him.

Many other animal rescue groups provide similar services. Specific breed groups rescue dogs of their own breed, while other rescue groups take in dogs of all breeds including mixed breeds. All of them are the good Samaritans of the dog world who provide safe havens for lost or abandoned dogs until loving and permanent homes can be found for them.

Since their adoption, Mac and Bo have blessed us with their love, joy, and faithful companionship. There is nothing they could ever do that would make us not love them. There is nothing they could ever do that would make us mistreat them. And there is nothing they could ever do that would make us abandon them or turn them over to somebody else.

We love Mac and Bo the way God loves us—unconditionally. He adopted us into His family for the same reasons we adopted Mac and Bo. He wanted to provide for us a loving environment where we can develop trust, rest in His mercy, and learn to walk with the Master.

God loves you unconditionally too. There is nothing you could ever think, say, or do that would make Him not love you. And He is the only one who can provide the hope, help, and healing for your deepest need.

Thank You, Father, for loving us so much that You want to adopt us into Your family. May dog lovers everywhere respond to Your love with joy.

The Lord is close to the brokenhearted and saves those who are crushed in spirit.

PSALM 34:18 NIV

DOING RESCUE WORK MEANS LOVING,
LEARNING, AND ACCEPTING EACH SITUATION.
IT'S EXHAUSTING AT TIMES AND HEARTBREAKING
AT OTHER TIMES; BUT MOSTLY RESCUE WORK
PROVIDES A GENUINE WARMTH IN BELIEVING
THAT A PERMANENT AND LOVING HOME
AWAITS EACH RESCUE.

CHRISTI COOPER

THE QUALITY OF A SOCIETY
WILL BE JUDGED ON HOW
THEY TREAT THEIR ANIMALS.

GANDHI

IF YOU CAN'T DECIDE
BETWEEN A SHEPHERD,
A SETTER, OR A POODLE,
GET THEM ALL . . . ADOPT A MUTT!

ASPCA

*Cast all your anxiety
on him because
he cares for you.*

1 PETER 5:7 NIV

LIFE WITH THE
GOOD MASTER

1

Bo: The Dog Who Needed Us

May the God of all grace, who called us
to His eternal glory by Christ Jesus,
after you have suffered a while, perfect,
establish, strengthen, and settle you.

1 PETER 5:10

Nine years ago while we were still grieving the death of our spaniel, I asked God to find just the right dog for us because we didn't want another one like lovable, but grouchy, Gus. While we had a puppy in mind, God had another plan. He knew the dog we needed; He knew the dog that needed us; and He began working all things for our good.

With winter coming on, a man who lived in the mountains called the English Springer Spaniel rescue club and said, "Come get Bo. I don't want him to have to spend another winter chained to a tree."

The rescue club sent Pete and Martha Dorland to pick him up. When they saw the thick collar and heavy metal chain holding back a black matted mass of dreadlocks, they approached Bo cautiously. But the closer they crept, the more they could see that the skinny little Springer who wiggled with happiness wasn't aggressive or hand-shy.

Bo smelled like a stagnant swamp when the Dorlands picked him up, placed him in their van, and drove him to the vet. There he was shaved, scrubbed, and neutered, and he even had his teeth cleaned. Amazingly Bo didn't have heartworms. The vet said the mats in his fur were so thick that parasite-carrying mosquitoes couldn't penetrate.

After his health check Bo's foster mom, Christi, drove him from the Atlanta vet to her home in Montgomery, Alabama, to learn how to live with a family.

Meanwhile I surfed the Internet in search of my next dog.

I kept running across breed rescue clubs, and logged on to learn more. A Web site for an organization in my own state indicated that Springers adopted through their rescue program were usually beyond the puppy stage. They had been examined by a vet, checked for heartworms, neutered, and given necessary shots. Additionally, they were temperament tested and usually house trained, obedience trained, crate trained, and trained to walk on a lead.

Wow! All the work was done, so our thoughts of a puppy vanished. Then we found out about Bo and began e-mailing Christi.

She said, "Bo has trachea damage from straining against the tie-out. I think he's deaf in one ear and blind on his left side from being hit by a car when he broke free one time. His left hindquarter is tender, too, but he's soft, sweet, and lovable."

Our hearts went out to Bo. We wanted to make up for his first five years, so we completed the necessary steps to adopt him and looked forward to restoring him to full health.

Bo entered his new life with us shortly after his fifth birthday and received our love with humility, thankfulness, and joy. He blossomed with every opportunity to obey, strut with a new toy, or claim my lap as his own.

His love, obedience, and faithfulness reminded me of the devotion that God desires from each of us. And through our love for Bo—meeting his physical and emotional needs while providing a safe environment where he could enjoy his freedom—we realized that God provided the same for us when He adopted us into His family. Then He heard our prayer and gave us the dog we needed in the dog who needed us.

> *We wait eagerly*
> *for our adoption . . .*
> *for in this hope,*
> *we were saved.*
>
> ROMANS 8:23–24 NIV

Heavenly Father, thank You for finding Bo for us. May he grow as strong, firm, and steadfast in our care as we have grown in Yours.

> IF YOU PICK UP A STARVING DOG
> AND MAKE HIM PROSPEROUS,
> HE WILL NOT BITE YOU. THAT IS THE PRINCIPAL
> DIFFERENCE BETWEEN A DOG AND A MAN.
>
> MARK TWAIN, PUDD'NHEAD WILSON'S CALENDAR

> HE IS YOUR FRIEND, YOUR PARTNER, YOUR DEFENDER,
> YOUR DOG. YOU ARE HIS LIFE, HIS LOVE,
> HIS LEADER. HE WILL BE YOURS, FAITHFUL AND TRUE,
> TO THE LAST BEAT OF HIS HEART. YOU OWE IT TO HIM
> TO BE WORTHY OF SUCH DEVOTION.
>
> UNKNOWN

A SECOND CHANCE. WOULDN'T IT BE NICE TO BE GIVEN A SECOND CHANCE AT LOVE? A RESCUE DOG LOOKS FOR JUST THAT OPPORTUNITY. A SECOND CHANCE TO SHOW LOVE AND UNDYING DEVOTION— A SECOND CHANCE TO LOVE AND BE LOVED.

CHRISTI COOPER

THE AVERAGE DOG IS A NICER PERSON THAN THE AVERAGE PERSON.

ANDREW A. ROONEY

2

Training at Camp Christi

Show me Your ways, O Lord;
Teach me Your paths.
Lead me in Your truth and teach me,
For You are the God of my salvation;
On You I wait all the day.

PSALM 25:4–5

Living with Christi must have been like a camp experience for Bo; so we dubbed her place "Camp Christi." For two weeks, Bo slept and napped in his own crate in a bunk room with other crated dogs—a far cry from his lonely crawlspace under a shed.

His first time in the yard, Bo walked around in a large circle as if he were still chained to the tree while his bunk buddies romped and played. By his second time out, he ran the entire area.

During his stay, Bo received some good home training. Christi, an obedience instructor, taught him to sit, stay, come, and walk on a leash. She sent us progress reports by e-mail. The first one read: "Bo is a bright little boy. He doesn't guard his food bowl or possessions, doesn't have a temperament problem, and he gets along well with other dogs. I am very encouraged by his enthusiasm and willingness to learn. And he loves getting fed on a regular basis. He has a big heart in spite of what he's been through and loves to be with people. Being tied out must have been very hard on him emotionally."

Christi trained Bo to sit and come using small pieces of hot dog as a reward. Then she took him to one of her obedience classes to learn how to walk on a loose leash and be petted by others.

Bo's leash training revealed the extent of his trachea damage. She wrote, "Initially we worked on just staying beside me. He tried desperately to understand, but could only take a few good steps before he started pulling at full strength again. The poor little guy was exhausted after a few minutes."

For the next session, she connected the leash to his collar and let him drag it around. At first, he took off full bolt, but when he realized there was nothing to pull against, he settled right into playing. She worked him up and down the hallway dragging his leash while she praised him and gave him treats, and of course she sent us progress reports.

Bo's leash training progressed with daily walks to the mailbox and less pulling each time. His second report card sounded like he had loosened up a lot: "This little guy loves to play with a tennis ball. When the ball was thrown, he wound up with it a good bit of the time. He doesn't bring it back. He trots along with it in his mouth and teases the other dogs. He has put on a couple of pounds and is starting to look healthier."

Christi let Bo in her house to acclimate him to indoor living and to housebreak him. It didn't take long. The first two times Bo started to sniff around and get himself into position to hike his leg, Christi walked him to the door and let him out. After that, when he needed to go, he walked around in a small circle. He had no accidents in the house, but he always wanted Christi to go out with him.

Christi's strength and courage to rescue, love, and train helpless Springers epitomizes the role of a foster mom. She said, "We want the next home for our rescues to be their last, and we are committed to doing all we can to ensure they are on their way to being good companions when they are placed."

That's exactly what we wanted for Bo. We wanted to be his next home and promised it would be his last.

Christi did for Bo what God does for us. He rescues us from the ways of the world; trains us to be good companions for Him; and shapes us with love, a gentle hand, and a promise to come get us and take us to the eternal home He has prepared for us.

Now it was time for us to take Bo home and fulfill our promise to him.

Heavenly Father, thank You for Christi and all the other foster parents who lovingly rescue and train our faithful pets. And thank You, Father, for all the people in our lives who come alongside us to train us and discipline us in the way that is most pleasing to You.

My child, never forget the things
I have taught you.
Store my commands in your heart.
If you do this, you will live many years,
and your life will be satisfying.
PROVERBS 3:1–2 NLT

*Take firm hold of instruction, do not let go;
Keep her, for she is your life.*

PROVERBS 4:13

IF A DOG WILL NOT COME TO YOU AFTER
HAVING LOOKED YOU IN THE FACE, YOU SHOULD
GO HOME AND EXAMINE YOUR CONSCIENCE.

WOODROW WILSON

Training Tips

RESCUE DOGS COME WITH BAGGAGE.
BUT WHO OF US DOESN'T? TRUE PEACE COMES
IN ACCEPTING THEIR LIMITATIONS, TEACHING
THEM THE BASICS, SHAPING WHERE APPROPRIATE,
AND ALWAYS BELIEVING THEY CAN BE RESTORED.

CHRISTI COOPER

WHEN WORKING WITH A RESCUE DOG, IT IS IMPORTANT
TO SHUT YOUR MOUTH AND OPEN YOUR EYES AND EARS.
THE DOG WILL GUIDE YOU WHERE THAT RELATIONSHIP NEEDS
TO JOURNEY. BELIEVE THEM, THEY ARE SO VERY HONEST.

CHRISTI COOPER

My Deliverer Is Coming

I am poor and needy;
Make haste to me, O God!
You are my help and my deliverer;
O LORD, do not delay.

PSALM 70:5

The day after Thanksgiving, just shy of Bo finishing two weeks at Camp Christi, we went to pick him up, looking forward to giving Bo the cushy life we promised. We felt like we knew him already; but Bo didn't know us, and he didn't know that we loved him. He only knew that Christi loved him, and we were concerned about suddenly tearing him away from the only love he knew.

Through countless e-mails we'd become good friends with Christi and looked forward to meeting her. I planned to hug her first thing for all she'd done for Bo, but she had another plan.

We pulled into her driveway, walked to the door, and rang her doorbell. Slowly the door opened, and I waited expectantly to see Christi's face appear. Instead, I felt a nose on my knee. When I looked down, there stood Bo.

All thoughts of Christi flew out the window as I went to my knees to greet him. He wiggled bashfully in my arms until I came to my senses and introduced myself to a laughing Christi.

Remembering that moment, Christi said later: "Bo had been very reserved with me because he was waiting for you. And when I opened the front door there was no question that Bo knew you had come for him. His message was profound. He wanted to be with you. There was nothing I would say or do to change that because we want each dog to go to the home destined for him."

I knew Bo was destined to be with us. He was God's answer to our prayer.

Christi led us through her house and out into her backyard to bond with Bo. She gave us all the time we needed for Bo to get used to us while he played, fetched, and strutted. When it was time to go, we signed the adoption papers and wrote out a check to the rescue group.

Christi fixed a goodie bag for us that included dog supply catalogs, canned and dry food, and even a leash to match Bo's collar. She also included a fleece sheep, a plush green gator, and a squeaky toy for Bo as adoption presents. She promised us continued support and wanted us to send her Bo tales.

We knew Christi had a soft spot in her heart for Bo, so we assured her that we loved him and would take good care of him. We walked to the car with Bo on his new leash and opened the door. Bo jumped right in as if he already knew it was his car. Christi smiled when Bo sat in my lap. She had put her heart into training him for this moment. Now that it had arrived, she turned to wipe tears of joy and sadness before she waved goodbye.

I hope we are as prepared and eager to enter our new life on the other side of eternity as Bo was to enter his new life with us. He knew a better day was coming, and he welcomed it. Do you?

Heavenly Father, Thank You for a new day coming. Prepare our hearts for Your glorious appearing.

I have come that they may have life, and that they may have it more abundantly.

JOHN 10:10

*Blessed is he who
considers the poor;
The LORD will deliver him
in time of trouble.*

PSALM 41:1

*Let us hold unswervingly
to the hope we profess, for
he who promised is faithful.*

HEBREWS 10:23 NIV

*The LORD is faithful
to all his promises
and loving toward
all he has made.*

PSALM 145:13 NIV

4

Old Habits Die Hard

Take My yoke upon you and learn from Me,
for I am gentle and lowly in heart,
and you will find rest for your souls.

MATTHEW 11:29

My husband has always said, "Everybody has their own little sack of rocks to tote," and Bo certainly had his when he came to live with us.

It was dark when we first brought Bo home, so we turned on the flood lights to help him adjust. Remnants of his years tied to a tree became apparent the instant we introduced him to our fenced backyard. Even though he had half an acre to explore, Bo had a full-blown anxiety attack, circling and panting heavily just like he did at Christi's.

Does he think we're going to tie him up again? I wondered.

I knelt beside him, drew him close to me, and held him until he calmed down.

"Bo, you don't need to circle anymore," I said, as if he understood. "No more tie-outs, no more straining against a chain, no more sleeping outside under an old shed. I promise you, Bo, you'll never be burdened again by being tied up. You can rest easy here. We're going to be good to you."

He slept in the bedroom with us that first night. The next morning when I let him out, he began circling again. So while he circled I walked to the nearest corner of the fence and called him.

"Bo, come."

He eyed me suspiciously as if he'd "come" several times before, and it hadn't worked out all that well for him.

I eased my way back over to him and slowly grasped Bo's collar to encourage him to explore the four corners of the yard with me. He yanked away from my grasp with surprising strength.

Bo's ingrained response to being tied caused him to pull, strain, or bolt against anything connected to his collar, even my hand.

I walked to a garden bench to wait while Bo continued circling within the restraint of his imagined chain. When he saw me sit down, he bolted in my direction as if anticipating the dreaded jerk of his chain. Surprised by the lack of resistance, he stumbled and fell forward, then scrambled to his feet and hurried to me.

"Good boy, Bo. You're free."

Back in the house I told him to "stay" while I went to check the mail. But the instant I opened the door, Bo bolted outside and ran down the driveway toward the road.

"Bo, come," I called, but he kept on running.

Then a strange thing happened. When Bo realized he was free, he stopped running away and frantically followed me back into the house, darting this way and that. He had experienced the effects of freedom twice in ten minutes and didn't know how to respond to it. So we knew our work was cut out for us.

In order for Bo to adjust to his newfound freedom it would be up to us to help him replace old habits with new ones.

It would be up to us to replace his fear with trust so he would come when called.

It would be up to us to lead him from the bondage of his circle to freedom in his new surroundings.

And it would be up to us to show our handsome, emotionally challenged, love-starved, one-eyed Bo the unconditional love it would take to make him whole.

That's what God does for us. He welcomes us into His family, carries our burdens, encourages our trust through His faithfulness, and draws us into His care with unselfish, unconditional, and undying love. And like Bo, when the moment comes that we realize we're free from that which has held us in bondage, we begin to trust and follow our Master. And in His presence we find rest for our weary souls.

Heavenly Father, My heart is at rest in Your presence. Thank You for setting Me free.

I have taught you in the way of wisdom;
I have led you in right paths.
When you walk, your steps will not be hindered,
and when you run, you will not stumble.

PROVERBS 4:11–12

TRY THAT BONE ON SOME OTHER DOG.

CERVANTES, DON QUIXOTE

EVERY RESCUE DOG NEEDS
A PERMANENT LOVING HOME
TO HELP HIM LEARN TO TRUST AGAIN.

CHRISTI COOPER

MONEY WILL BUY A FINE DOG BUT
ONLY KINDNESS WILL MAKE HIM WAG HIS TAIL.

AUTHOR UNKNOWN

I HAVE A DOG OF BLENHEIM BIRTH,
WITH FINE LONG EARS AND FULL OF MIRTH;
AND SOMETIMES, RUNNING O'ER THE PLAIN,
HE TUMBLES ON HIS NOSE:
BUT QUICKLY JUMPING UP AGAIN,
LIKE LIGHTNING ON HE GOES!

JOHN RUSKIN, "MY DOG DASH"

5

Separation Anxiety

Who shall separate us from the love of Christ? . . .
I am persuaded that neither death nor life, nor angels
nor principalities nor powers, nor things present
nor things to come, nor height nor depth, nor any
other created thing, shall be able to separate us from
the love of God which is in Christ Jesus our Lord.

ROMANS 8:35, 38–39

During Bo's first week with us, we managed our schedules so that one of us was at home with him at all times. We enjoyed watching him relish his newfound freedom. He galloped across the yard to pounce on a thrown ball, carried it with one cheek slobbered over the side, and strutted back only to tease us and turn away.

He sat with us on the couch and let us snack without begging for a bite. He never growled or showed any signs of aggression when we played with him, tugged on his toys, or placed a hand near his food bowl. He was a combination of all the good traits of all our dogs in the last thirty years.

Bo even conducted "bed check" to make sure we were still there when the lights were turned off. He came to my side of the bed and nudged my elbow.

"I'm here, Bo."

Then went around to the other side to nudge Earl's elbow.

"I'm here, too, Bo."

Comforted by our presence, he went to his bed nearby and slept there all night.

That was Bo's nightly routine for months until he believed in our faithfulness to be where he hoped we would be. Some nights he even slept in the bed with us to make sure.

Bo loved us so much he followed us from room to room and curled up to sleep wherever we were. His symptoms of separation anxiety—a panic response to being separated from us—started out so subtly that we didn't even notice. We thought it was cute the way he followed us. After all, we adopted him to be a companion dog, and he certainly lived up to his job title.

Although he'd been crate-trained at Christi's, we didn't have a crate, so the first time I left Bo alone I put him in the bathroom where clean-up, if needed, would be easier. Then I secured a gate in place instead of closing the door. When I returned thirty minutes later I found Bo sound asleep on the living room couch. He had knocked down the gate, trotted down the hall, and lifted all the floor length blinds in the living room to look outside for me.

Then we discovered Bo had a problem with any barrier that kept him away from us. Outdoors, when we worked in the outer yard and left him inside the fence, Bo ran up and down the fence barking and trying to bite through the chain links. Indoors, when I put him in the bathroom with a gate, he knocked down the gate to reach us. When we bought a crate, he turned it over and escaped out the bottom, then chewed through the wires of another one. But when I left him in the bathroom with the door closed, full blown madness possessed his kind and gentle soul.

I returned to find the bathroom floor littered with splinters, paint chips, cosmetics, prescriptions, and clothes. Everything that had hung on the back of my door was ripped to shreds. He scratched the paint off the door and door jamb, gnawed to splinters the entire width of the bottom of the solid wood door, and scraped the wallpaper off the wall next to the door. Then he grabbed a tray on the back of the countertop, yanked it to the floor, and chewed up my makeup bag.

He stripped and shredded a roll of toilet paper, pulled the blinds down off the window, and excreted two huge piles which he stepped in and smeared all over the floor, walls, door, bath towels, and blinds. And after all that, he somehow opened the door, jumped up on our bed, and collapsed from exhaustion. He continued to snore while I examined the carnage.

Was I angry? Yes, but only over the circumstances of his former life that had brought him to this point. We felt nothing but love and compassion for this poor, pitiful pup. We knew that he had acted out of fear of losing the love he'd finally found, and we vowed to love him and care for him the rest of his days.

Bo continued to follow me from room to room and sleep at my feet wherever I was. I started leaving him for brief periods of time, often standing just right outside the door, to desensitize him to being separated from me. Our only concern was where to leave him when both of us were gone.

After much discussion on how to solve the problem we theorized that because we always found him sound asleep on the couch or on our bed after each escape, he might be more comfortable with free reign of the house instead of limiting his freedom. As a test case I left him alone in the house for thirty minutes.

In my absence Bo separated the blinds to peek out, pulled a bag of muffins off the counter in the kitchen, and turned on the stove.

Those were problems we could handle. We removed food from the countertops and threw the switch to the stove every time we left so our counter-surfing spaniel wouldn't accidentally burn down the house.

After that, Bo slept or paced in our absence. When we returned, we always heard his soft, mournful moan until the key turned in the lock. The instant the door opened and he saw us, his countenance turned to pure, hyperventilating joy.

Bo threw his head back and sang, woooo-woo-woo which I interpreted to mean, "I am not alone for my master is with me."

I know how Bo feels. Don't you?

My anxiety turns to unabashed joy when I'm in the presence of my Master. It's the joy of knowing that I still have His love, mercy, and forgiveness regardless of the mess I've made. In His presence I find what we're all looking for:

> Joy beyond measure,
> Rest for my soul,
> And the love of my Master
> To make me whole.

Bo knocked down gates, opened doors, and escaped cages to get closer to his master.

Aren't you glad that nothing can separate us from ours?

Heavenly Father, thank You for a love so powerful that it can demolish all barriers.

For he (Jesus) himself is our peace . . .
and has destroyed the barrier.

EPHESIANS 2:14 NIV

DOGS ARE NOT OUR WHOLE LIFE,
BUT THEY MAKE OUR LIVES WHOLE.

ROGER CARAS

6

Harnessed, Not Shackled

Now I will break off his yoke from you,
and burst your bonds apart.

NAHUM 1:13

Bo's raspy, muffled bark clearly told us he had trachea damage from all those years of pulling against the chain that bound him to a tree. Every time he walked on a leash, he remembered those days and continued to pull, further aggravating his throat. So we measured the depth of his chest and bought him a harness to use instead of a collar.

The minute his collar was removed, Bo shook all over, threw his head back, and pursed his lips in praise.

Woo-woo-woo-o-o-o!

The shackles were gone.

Then together Bo and I figured out how to dress him in his new blue harness. Relieved of the pressure of a collar against his throat, Bo shook the harness into a comfortable position and pranced around the room. His harness stretched across his strong chest and shoulders, eliminated further damage to his throat, and gave it an opportunity to heal. It also allowed Bo to cut more of the mental ties of bondage to the past. His leash attached to a ring on the top of his harness and shifted the pressure from his throat to his shoulders. The more we walked together, the more he realized he was tethered to me in a bond of love.

Slowly he began to respond. When he heard me pick up his leash, saw me kneel down to his level, and open my arms to him, he learned that "come" meant reward, not punishment.

He knew that even though he voluntarily let himself be tethered again, I was right there to lead him on to a new adventure. His leash became to him the tie that bound us together and allowed Bo the freedom to walk with his master.

That's what the Lord has done for us. He has broken our bondage to past sins and guilt and tethered us to Himself in a bond of love that is no longer painful, injurious, or isolating. And we know that when we hear His voice in our spirit say, "Come," we have received an invitation to walk with our Master in freedom.

Heavenly Father, thank You for breaking My yoke of bondage and setting Me free.

Stand fast therefore in the liberty
by which Christ has made us free,
and do not be entangled again
with a yoke of bondage.

GALATIANS 5:1

Fetch

Because you love him, consider replacing your dog's collar with an adjustable harness to prevent choking. For a proper fit, measure around his chest, behind his front legs.

Training Tips

Trust is a big issue with rescues. Kneel, open your arms, and say, "Come." Then praise him for his obedience.

Bow Down Before Me

I love the early morning quiet of being the first one up. If Bo isn't curled up in bed with us, I make my way to the kitchen, checking out his favorite sleeping spots as I go.

Although I can't see him, I sense his presence and turn to see him padding softly toward me. I stoop to welcome him into my arms. He lowers his ears, pauses in front of me to bow down (and stretch) in humble recognition of my authority over him. Then he cuddles into my embrace to receive the love I have for him.

Do you start the day in humble recognition of your Master? He waits for you with open arms.

7

Walking with the Master

Can two walk together, unless they are agreed?

AMOS 3:3

My husband and I both walked Bo on a leash—sometimes together and sometimes separately. When Bo walked with Earl, he learned to keep up and stay focused. Those walks were for exercise, burning calories, and expending energy. Walking with Earl meant conforming to his exercise regimen. When Bo walked with me, he took time to smell the flowers and examine each blade of grass that caught his fancy. He had the time and freedom he needed to leisurely explore the world around him while safely tethered to me.

Through the consistency of our intentions, Bo learned what to expect when walking with each of us. It didn't matter to him whether he walked in obedience or walked in freedom. As long as he walked with one of us tethered to the other end of the leash, Bo was happy.

When he saw us pick up his leash or heard the click of the clasp, he knew he was going. He ran to us, sat at our feet shimmering with excitement, and started singing praises— Woo-woo-woo-o-o-o!

Like Bo, we have been set free to walk with our Master. When we walk with Him in obedience, He directs our steps and conforms us to His will. And when we walk with Him in freedom, we can relax knowing that we are right where He wants us, protected by His mighty power along the way. Doesn't that make you want to sing His praises for the privilege?

Bo grew from being afraid of the tether to excitedly antici-pating it. He learned that he could love us knowing that his love was returned, trust us without fear of being abandoned, and depend upon us to be faithful to him.

That's what God wants us to know about Him. He loves us, He's worthy of our trust, and He's dependable. In good times and bad He stretches out His mighty hand and saves us for Himself so we can walk with Him in obedience and in freedom.

Heavenly Father, what a joy it is to walk with You in freedom every day.

Do not be conformed to this world, but be transformed by the renewing of your mind, that you may prove what is that good and acceptable and perfect will of God.

ROMANS 12:2

48

*Now the Lord
is the Spirit,
and where the Spirit
of the Lord is,
there is freedom.*

2 CORINTHIANS 3:17 NIV

MAN IS A DOG'S IDEA
OF WHAT GOD SHOULD BE.

HOLBROOK JACKSON

8

Anxiously Pacing

When anxiety was great within me,
Your consolation brought joy to my soul.

PSALM 94:19 NIV

To this day I feel blessed that my neighbor left his brush pile smoldering. A swirling wind fanned the flame out of control, and by the time I looked out the kitchen window and discovered a smoke-filled backyard, we'd lost two of our three wooded acres.

The fire department and forestry commission bulldozed a firebreak around the burning area to contain the fire. That firebreak became my walking trail through the woods.

After a good rain doused the smoldering underbrush, Bo and I walked the trail. We discovered that it joined the easement road along the back of our property and gave us a long walk in the woods to enjoy the quiet freedom of God's creation. We walked that trail every day, sometimes twice.

I didn't leash Bo on our walks in the woods. He liked to run the deer trails, and I liked to watch him run free. Although his separation anxiety wouldn't let him stay gone long, I usually made it home first and watched out the kitchen window for him to burst into the clearing. With ears flying, he ran for the pure joy of running.

One day he strayed farther from me than usual on our walk. I whistled and called him occasionally, but he didn't come, so I prayed for his safe return and headed to the house.

When I walked out of the woods bordering the deepest part of our yard, I saw Bo already standing on the deck. He peeked through the full-length window in the back door to see if I was inside.

My brief, shrill whistle pierced the air to let him know that I was on the way.

Bo's head jerked around in the direction of the sound, but he didn't see me. I was still too far away for his poor vision, so he returned his attention to the back door. Normally I was in the house by the time he returned from our walks in the woods, so he hesitated to give up his post. As I got closer, a second whistle brought the same response. He didn't see me and paced anxiously on the deck.

From sixty yards away, I whistled a third time. He jerked his head around far enough to see a figure approaching, but he couldn't identify me. Slowly he walked down the deck steps and turned in my direction. He stopped, not knowing who was approaching. I stopped too, to let him recognize me, but he still had no clue. Then I knelt on one knee and held out my arms. With instant recognition, Bo walked sheepishly toward me until he wiggled joyfully in my presence.

Isn't that just like us? We follow our own desires and wind up in a panic when we realize we're not where we want to be. The farther we move away from the Lord, the more the world clouds our vision so that we don't even recognize Him. Then out of His great love for us He makes His presence more recognizable. He meets us on our own level.

Are you where you want to be, or are you on the verge of panic knowing that you've strayed from God's presence? Are you pacing anxiously on the deck of your life?

In an anxious moment, Bo walked back into my presence and found joy, comfort, and peace when I welcomed him with open arms. When you seek God's presence, you'll find Him waiting for you, too, and His comfort will bring joy to your soul.

Heavenly Father, You fill me with joy in Your presence and comfort me with peace.

You have made known
to me the ways of life;
You will make me full of joy
in Your presence.

ACTS 2:28

IN THE PRESENCE OF JEHOVAH,
GOD ALMIGHTY, PRINCE OF PEACE,
TROUBLES VANISH, HEARTS ARE MENDED
IN THE PRESENCE OF THE KING.

CATHY GODDARD

TO LOVE A DOG
THAT HAS BEEN DISCARDED
BY ANOTHER PROVES
TO THAT DOG THAT LOVE
REALLY DOES EXIST.

CHRISTI COOPER

9

How Closely Do You Follow Your Master?

For His merciful kindness is great toward us,
and the truth of the LORD endures forever.

PSALM 117:2

Bo knows when I'm getting ready to leave the house. He follows me from room to room as I gather the things I need to take with me. It's as if he doesn't want to miss one minute with me. When I start down the hall, his nose brushes against my right calf every step until I turn and say, "Stay."

Then he sits next to the wall and leans to his right to watch me walk the rest of the way to the door. There he waits patiently for my voice and the word he longs to hear: "Okay." When I say it, Bo's countenance changes immediately. He sprints to the door with such excited happiness he can hardly contain himself. He screeches to a halt, then wiggles, dances, and talks all at once. Woo-woo-woo-woo-woo, he sings as if he's praising me just for letting him go along.

But most of the time Bo doesn't get to accompany me. And when I return home, I often find him pacing from room to room mourning my absence with a long, low, soul wrenching wail. It was during one of those times that Bo's faithfulness to me sparked questions about my faithfulness to my Master.

Do I follow my Master so closely that I could almost reach out and touch Him?

Do I keep my eyes focused on Him?

Do I wait patiently and listen intently for His Voice?

Am I attentive when He speaks to me?

Am I full of joy when I enter into His presence?

Do I mourn His absence when I've separated myself from Him?

I'm so thankful that my Master always wants me with Him. He always draws me closer. There's never a time when He would say, "Stay. You can't go with Me today."

There's never a time when He would shut me out from His presence. If He did, I'd feel abandoned just like Bo feels when I leave him.

Thankfully, God promises us, "The LORD your God is a merciful God, He will not forsake you nor destroy you" (Deuteronomy 4:31).

But God must feel abandoned when I choose not to follow Him. He must feel abandoned knowing that Bo is more loyal to me than I am to Him, and He must be grieved when I fail to follow wherever He leads, because the Bible says, "Do not grieve the Holy Spirit" (Ephesians 4:30).

So today, I'm going to keep my eyes fixed on Jesus, my Master.

Today, I'm going to wait patiently and listen intently for His Voice.

Today, I'm going to rejoice in His presence.

And today, I'm going to hug Bo and thank him for his faithfulness.

Heavenly Father, thank You for Your faithfulness and Your promise never to abandon Me. Open My eyes so I can see You more clearly. Open My ears to be more receptive to Your Voice. And open My heart to rejoice in Your presence.

MY LITTLE OLD DOG:
A HEART-BEAT
AT MY FEET.

EDITH WHARTON

*Therefore know that the LORD your God,
He is God, the faithful God who keeps covenant
and mercy for a thousand generations with those
who love Him and keep His commandments.*

DEUTERONOMY 7:9

HISTORIES ARE MORE FULL
OF EXAMPLES OF THE FIDELITY
OF DOGS THAN OF FRIENDS.

ALEXANDER POPE

10

Victory Over Death

Preserve my life, for I am holy;
You are my God;
Save Your servant who trusts in You! . . .
For great is Your mercy toward me,
and You have delivered my soul
from the depths of Sheol.

PSALM 86:2, 13

When Bo and I walked the trail through the woods, I always stayed on the path, but Bo often followed his nose wherever it led. One day, it led him into trouble.

I had just finished walking the back trail and made the turn to start the long trail home when Bo took a shortcut to catch up with me. Suddenly I heard him yelp.

He ran to me with a swarm of fierce, angry yellow jackets all over him. I swatted at them with bare hands, stripping them off his rump, legs, and the back of his ears until they were all gone. By then Bo had been stung so many times his legs were weak. I grabbed his harness to help him along, knowing that I couldn't carry him all the way home. He had to walk as far as he could.

By the time we stumbled out of the woods together, Bo panted heavily and drooled like a Saint Bernard in the heat of summer. I picked him up, put him in the car, and called the vet to tell him we were on the way. When we arrived, Bo had lapsed into a deep sleep, so I carried him into the vet's office.

The vet immediately gave him an injection of dexamethasone.

"It's a good thing you brought him in," he said. "He could have died from that many stings."

Five minutes later Bo opened his eyes.

"He'll be fine now," the vet assured me.

On the drive home I realized Bo had cheated death through the work of our vet just like Jesus defeated death through the power of His resurrection. Because Jesus lives, we will too.

Quietly I sang "Because He Lives," filling the cab of the car with gratitude.

The victory we have over death far exceeds Bo's victory over the yellow jackets. The Bible says when we reach the other side of eternity we will be so filled with joy that we will leap like calves. Bo must have thought that was a good idea too. He was wide awake when I pulled into the garage and opened the car door for him. He leaped out of the car, pounced on his stuffed pink pig, and strutted around the house in celebration of his new lease on life.

Father, You promised that the present order of things will pass away, and there will be no more death or mourning or crying or pain. Thank You for giving us victory over death through the resurrection of Your Son.

Fetch

Keep Benadryl® on hand for minor bee stings. If the dog has any difficulty breathing after a sting (a true allergic reaction) get them to a veterinarian immediately. Do not try to treat this yourself.

CHRISTI COOPER, LPN

But for you who revere my name,
the sun of righteousness will rise
with healing in its wings.
And you will go out and leap
like calves released from the stall.

MALACHI 4:2 NIV

Back on the Path

Bo held his head high, sniffed the wind and strayed off the path into the woods where the rotting carcass of a small animal lay. The stench attracted his attention every time we reached that point in our walk.

I followed him a few steps, grabbed the top of his harness and turned him around to walk on the path with me. When we passed that area on our way back to the house, Bo left the path again to follow his desires. This time, I picked up a small stick and whacked him on the behind.

God does the same thing for us, because He disciplines those He loves. When you feel His loving hand of discipline on your life, how will you respond?

11

Take It to the Dump

Cast your burden on the LORD,
and He shall sustain you;
He shall never permit
the righteous to be moved.

PSALM 55:22

Over the years my dogs have inspired many life lessons for me. Bo chose one Christmas to reinforce the lesson of accepting responsibility instead of looking for someone else to blame. What I had planned as a head start on the next day's chores, Bo saw as an invitation to do what dogs do.

Twas the night before dump day and all through the house,
A creature was stirring, but it wasn't a mouse.
With trash bags filled full and arranged by the door,
I should have known better, I should have thought more.

But I went on to bed for a sound night of sleep,
And heard not a thing, not even a peep;
Till morn rolled around and husband yelled, "Hon!
Get in here now. See what your dog's done!"

Paper was shredded, tin cans licked clean,
Litter and garbage in three rooms was seen.
But where was the dog? I looked everywhere.
Then I noticed him hiding under a chair.

I rolled a newspaper and almost was cursin',
Whopping myself and yelling, "Bad Person!"
But the mess is cleaned up now; the dog's in my lap;
And we've settled in for that long winter's nap.

Bo had sniffed and rooted through the garbage for scraps, and I paid the consequences for leaving it parked by the door.

That morning as I knelt to pick up each little piece that littered the living room, dining room, and kitchen, God spoke to my heart. *While you're down there, let's talk.*

He showed me that my heart was littered with garbage too. Blaming others when the fault was my own; hanging on to old hurts; harboring bitterness when life didn't seem fair; allowing petty annoyances to mushroom into full-blown anger.

"Lord, take these from me," I prayed. "I don't want them cluttering my heart."

Cast your cares on the LORD, and he will sustain you (Psalm 55:22 NIV).

"Empty me of myself so I can see You more clearly."

Cast your cares on the LORD, and he will sustain you.

"Cleanse me of all unrighteousness."

Cast your cares on the LORD, and he will sustain you.

By the time I had cleaned up the mess, I had cast all my cares, burdens, and problems on the Lord.

With my burden lifted, I drove to the dump thinking, *His yoke is indeed easy, and His burden is light.*

At the dump I opened the trunk, grabbed those bags of garbage and hurled them into the bin just like God hurls all our iniquities into the depths of the sea. Then I drove away and left them there.

Now when I go from room to room gathering the garbage, I start with the room in my heart and clean it as I go along. I ask God to reveal to me any issue that He and I have not addressed, any sin I have not confessed, any duty I have shirked. As He brings my heart garbage to mind, I confess it, ask forgiveness for it, and then bag it, so I can take it to the dump and leave it there before it stinks up my life.

Do you have heart garbage you need to take to the dump? Let's come clean this Christmas and haul it all to the dump so we can celebrate the birth of our Savior with a pure heart. Let's sing joyfully to the world because the Lord has come, and we have received our King.

King Jesus. The only One who can take a dog's mess and turn it into a life lesson.

Heavenly Father, thank You for teaching me to cast my cares on You and leave them with You. Thank You for reminding me that when You hurl my confessed sins into the depths of the sea, You remember them no more. Help me to do the same.

Cocoa Bo

Bo slept peacefully beside me while I sat on the floor filling Christmas mugs with packs of cocoa mix. When I ran out of packs, I went to the kitchen for another box. Two minutes later, that black and white spaniel—that former junkyard dog—greeted me with a chocolate grin, a chocolate chest, and chocolate paws. Hence the saying, "To err is human, to forgive, canine."

Who is a God like You,
pardoning iniquity
and passing over the transgression
of the remnant of His heritage?
He does not retain His anger forever,
because He delights in mercy.
He will again have compassion on us,
and will subdue our iniquities.

Micah 7:18–19

12

Waiting Patiently

The LORD is not slow in keeping his promise,
as some understand slowness.
He is patient with you . . . wanting
everyone to come to repentance.

2 PETER 3:9 NIV

Every trip to the woods was a new adventure. Bo kept his nose to the ground eager to pick up the scent of a deer and run wherever his nose led him.

While Bo followed his own pleasure, I finished my walk and waited for him at the top of the hill. I loved the view from there, especially in the fall. With fewer leaves on the trees, I could see farther as I watched for Bo and prayed for his safe return.

The sound of falling leaves, nuts crashing to the forest floor, and woodpeckers banging bark for bugs broke the silence. Then, in the distance, I heard Bo running fast and breathing hard. I scanned the woods from my vantage point without seeing him, so I looked for movement.

Ah. Over there. Still a hundred yards away but back on the path with his nose to the ground, Bo stopped where the trails crossed. He sniffed the air for direction then followed the path laid out for him long ago. He ran full speed up the winding path.

On his final turn, he saw me waiting. His pace slowed as he walked humbly into my presence. I stooped down to welcome him.

"Good boy, Bo. I'm so glad you came back."

He threw out his chest, laid his ears back, and strutted by my side all the way back to the house, thankful he found me and relieved that he didn't get scolded for running off.

Many times, we're just like Bo. We leave God's intended path to pursue our own selfish interests. Then at some point we realize that we moved too far off the path and begin to find our way back. But God promised that He would never leave us or forsake us, and thankfully, He is faithful to His promise.

If you've turned to the right or to the left and wandered off the path that God laid out for you, be still and listen for His voice. You might hear Him say, "This is the way, walk in it" (Isaiah 30:21).

Once Bo found his way back to the path, he found me waiting for him. When you find your way back to God's path, you, too, will be happy, thankful, and relieved to find your Master right where you left Him, praying for you, and waiting patiently for your return so He can walk you home.

Father, You are so patient as You wait for us to return to You. Thank You for Your faithfulness even when we are not faithful.

*Your ears shall hear a word behind you, saying,
"This is the way, walk in it,"
whenever you turn to the right hand
or whenever you turn to the left.*

ISAIAH 30:21

What's On Your Mind?

One morning as Bo and I walked in the woods, I could hear a herd of deer to my right running parallel to our path. Because Bo is deaf in one ear, he didn't hear them, but he picked up their scent where the deer crossed our path about fifty yards ahead.

Suddenly, Bo stiffened, sniffed the air a few times, then took off in the opposite direction. He always wants to know where the deer have been, so he backtracks and eliminates all possibilities before following the freshest scent. It's a predictable behavior to me because I know Bo.

You probably know your dog as well as I know mine, but did you know that God knows you even better than you know your dog? He knows what you are going to do in any given circumstance before the thought ever crosses your mind, and He loves you anyway. Why don't you take a minute to thank God for all that He is and all that He does in your life? And thank Him for loving you in spite of all that crosses your mind.

Your word is a lamp to my feet
and a light to my path.

PSALM 119:105

13

When Faith Falters

*So [Jesus] said, "Come." And when Peter had come down
out of the boat, he walked on the water to go to Jesus.
But when he saw that the wind was boisterous, he was afraid;
and beginning to sink he cried out, saying, "Lord, save me!"
And immediately Jesus stretched out His hand and caught him.*

MATTHEW 14:29–31

Bo loves to go to the lake, not to swim, but to ride in the boat. He loves jumping from the dock into the boat. He loves the feel of the wind in his face, and he loves jumping back out of the boat onto the dock.

Sometimes after a boat ride he gets so excited he can't wait to spring onto the dock—like the time he strained at his leash in eagerness to make the jump.

"Stay," I commanded, knowing there was too much water between the boat and the dock for a successful jump. But Bo pulled so hard, I decided to let him go for it.

Many times when we are headstrong, God will let us have our own way too. Even though He knows what's best for us, He will allow us to make our own decisions even when they are bad ones.

Bo's decision was a bad one.

His front feet landed safely on the dock, but his back feet pushed the boat farther away, and he didn't get enough "push" to complete the jump.

Whoomph!

His belly slammed into the side of the dock and knocked the wind out of him. Clinging for life, his toenails raked desperately into the wooden boards, while his body sank into the lake. Quickly I reached down, grabbed the top of his harness, and lifted him out of the water and back into the boat.

That's what God does for us. He lifts us up from the watery grave of bad decisions and hauls us back to safety when we cry out, "Lord, save me!" like Peter did.

The circumstances of Peter and Bo are much like our own. Jesus beckoned Peter to come to Him, and Bo was beckoned by his own desire to jump onto the dock. Both obeyed the beckoning and got out of the boat. Peter acted in faith and experienced the power of God. But Bo took a leap of faith in himself and experienced his own lack of power. Peter lost his focus, and his faith in God faltered. Bo lost his footing, and his faith in himself faltered. Both started out with good intentions, but both landed in the drink. Then, Jesus reached out His hand and caught Peter, and I reached down and caught Bo. Both were pulled to safety.

Jesus is always on standby to pull us to safety, too, in hopes that after a lifesaving experience, we will respond the same way as those who were in the boat with Peter. They worshiped Jesus, saying, "Truly You are the Son of God," (Matthew 14:33).

And I give them eternal life, and they shall never perish;
neither shall anyone snatch them out of My hand.
My Father, who has given them to Me, is greater than all;
and no one is able to snatch them out of My Father's hand.

JOHN 10:28–29

Heavenly Father, thank You for Your constant presence and for always knowing what's best for us. Remind us that we need not fear the trials of this life, because You always listen for the cry of our hearts so You can reach down and pull us to safety.

"Surely this is our God;
we trusted in him, and he saved us.
This is the LORD, we trusted in him;
let us rejoice and be glad in his salvation."

ISAIAH 25:9 NIV

Fetch

Because you love him, put a life jacket on your dog when boating or swimming. Yes, he can swim, but he can also drown under the same conditions that would drown you.

Fear not, for I am with you;
Be not dismayed, for I am your God.
I will strengthen you,
yes, I will help you,
I will uphold you
with My righteous right hand.

ISAIAH 41:10

14

Obedient to My Voice

If you love Me, keep My commandments.

JOHN 14:15

I've heard people say, "I love my dogs more than I love most people."
On some days I agree with them, and God took me to task over it as Bo and I
stood in the garage watching the steady downpour of a much needed rain.

I was startled out of my thoughts when Bo—who doesn't even like to get
his toes wet—made a mad dash in that heavy rain to retrieve his knotted sock
lying in the driveway. Then he turned and sprinted for the door.

While his wet feet slid on the slick garage floor, I glanced at the kitchen
door. It was open just enough for Bo to nudge his way in. Instantly I visualized
the mop up I would have to do if he shook that wet sock all over the house.

"Stay," I commanded, knowing I couldn't get there before his nose nudged
the door open.

Bo screeched to a halt on the top doorstep. He turned and looked at me
with that soggy sock dangling from his mouth.

"Drop it."

He lowered his chin and opened his mouth. The sock splatted on the step.

"Good boy, Bo."

I walked toward the door silently thanking God for Bo's obedience.

As I hugged and praised Bo, my heart quickened as if I heard God say, *Oh,
that you would be as obedient to My voice as Bo is to yours.*

Guilty as charged.

Father, I know You have something specific in mind. What is it? I asked as I pondered our brief but silent conversation.

Later that afternoon our conversation continued when I read, "This is My commandment, that you love one another as I have loved you" (John 15:12).

I read the last part again. "As I have loved you."

In other words, not like you love. Love like I love.

Oh. That kind of love.

Finally it made sense to me. I had always read, "Love your neighbor as yourself." And to be honest, there are times when I don't love myself all that much, so I couldn't understand why God would want me to love somebody else like that.

The quiet voice said, *Your lack of understanding doesn't excuse your disobedience.*

Gulp. Sometimes truth can be hard to swallow, but I'm hardheaded, so I pressed the issue. "Lord, what about the other person? They tend to love on their terms like, 'I'll love you if . . .' or 'I'll love you when . . . .' Their love is conditional."

Love them anyway. I loved you while you were unlovable. I loved you with an everlasting love. They need for you to show them what My kind of love looks like.

"You mean love them first?"

You loved your dog first, didn't you? Maybe if I had said, "Love your neighbor as much as you love your dog," you would have gotten the idea.

"You're right. That might have made more since to me. I am patient and kind to Bo. I love on him all the time, protect him at all costs, and meet all his needs. I would never abandon him. He's my forever friend. I love him unconditionally."

That's the way I want you to love people.

"Even though some people are unlovable?"

Especially the ones who are unlovable. You keep forgetting that I loved you when you were unlovable, and I still do.

Yes, but You are God. How can I love the unlovable?

You can love them because I first loved you.

You did, didn't You, Lord?

Did Bo return your love when you loved him first?

Yes, Lord.

Did Bo obey you because he loves you?

Yes, Lord.

In the same way, if you love Me, you will obey what I command.

Yes, Lord.

Then "Love one another. As I have loved you, so you must love one another" (John 13:34 NIV).

> LOVE ME,
> LOVE MY DOG.
> JOHN HEYWOOD

Heavenly Father, thank You for your love and Your patience. Grant us the power to know and understand the width, height, length, and depth of Your love for us so we can love others the way You love us.

For God so loved the world that He gave His only begotten Son, that whoever believes in Him should not perish but have everlasting life.

JOHN 3:16

15

Mac: A Sweet Spirit

You called in trouble, and I delivered you.

PSALM 81:7

Bo was eleven years old when we started thinking about getting another dog. We had always had two at a time until Bo entered our lives, but he was so love-starved we kept putting it off. "It wouldn't be fair to Bo," we said.

Every time that conversation came up, we tabled the issue—until Christi, Bo's foster mom, e-mailed us about Mac.

She said, "English Springer Spaniel Rescue in Atlanta just took in another Springer. He has a sweet spirit, and they wondered if you were ready for another one."

Isn't it amazing how God works? He'd already prepared our hearts through many conversations about getting another dog, and now He had not only prepared the right dog, but the right people to make the connection. He worked all things for our good, the dog's good, and the good of the rescue people. Isn't God good!

So while Bo was the answer to our prayers, we were about to become the answer to someone else's prayers for Mac.

We e-mailed Christi that we would think about it and asked how he wound up as a rescue. She said his early years were unknown, but Mac was found lying beside a busy street in Atlanta with a debilitating hip injury from being hit by a car. A compassionate lady, who recognized him as a Springer and knew a friend involved in English Springer Spaniel Rescue, saw him and took him to her vet. With his hip socket repaired, he was placed in a foster home while his hip healed and a massive search for his owner continued. After six weeks with no owner coming forward, we were contacted, and we soon made arrangements to meet Mac.

With boundless energy and ears flying, Mac ran to greet us from deep in the backyard. He came to a screeching halt at our feet. Then he turned his attention to Bo while Earl and I watched him.

Unlike Bo's perfectly chiseled, block forehead, and square muzzle, Mac's head was as pointy as his thin muzzle. And in stark contrast to Bo's small, stocky, athletic build, Mac stood a full hand taller and all out of proportion with small shoulders and a big rear end. As far as his looks went, the only attribute we didn't object to was his chocolate and white coat, even though Bo was black and white.

"He's not the handsomest dog in the lot," I said, realizing how shallow I sounded as I recalled that the Lord looks at the heart.

We had just about decided that Mac wasn't right for us when he turned, walked over to my husband sitting on a bench, and kissed him.

"Okay, this one's my dog," Earl said.

With one heart in his favor, I decided to give Mac a second look while he ran over to play with Bo. When Bo ignored him, Mac jumped on him. Bo growled and snapped, but Mac jumped back without retaliating then ran a big circle around Bo and bumped him again as he buzzed by.

Bo snapped and growled again, but Mac didn't fight back. Then it happened a third time with no fight resulting.

"That's a positive. At least he's not a fighter. Come here, Mac," I called. As I cupped his muzzle in my hands, I noticed a skin tag on his left lower lid. Not a problem either, I thought, but we left undecided.

When Mac reinjured his hip and needed another surgery to repair it, his recovery gave us six more weeks to think about him. I admitted that I was impressed by Mac's sweet spirit, so we arranged another visit.

Our second visit was like the first. Mac tried to get Bo to play with him, Bo snapped and growled, and Mac jumped back without retaliating. His playfulness without aggression was a huge plus in his favor, so I knelt and called him to me.

He came immediately, sat down in front of me, and looked me squarely in the eye.

"Mac, do you want to go home with us?"

I don't know what I expected in response, but when Mac bowed his head and leaned against my leg, my heart pumped in his favor, too. I put my arm around his shoulders and called Bo to me. His response would be the final test. Bo walked over and sat down beside Mac. I couldn't believe it. There they sat—two males side by side, neither vying for attention, nor trying to push the other one out. So with Bo's approval, Mac became a member of our family.

Heavenly Father, thank You for working all angles to bring Mac into our family.

*And we know that all things
work together for good
to those who love God,
to those who are the called
according to His purpose.*

ROMANS 8:28

*"The LORD does not look
at the things man looks at.
Man looks at the outward appearance,
but the LORD looks at the heart."*

1 SAMUEL 16:7 NIV

A DOG IS NOT "ALMOST HUMAN,"
AND I KNOW OF NO GREATER INSULT
TO THE CANINE RACE THAN
TO DESCRIBE IT AS SUCH.

JOHN HOLMES

16

Brotherly Love

*How good and pleasant it is when
brothers live together in unity!*

PSALM 133:1 NIV

There were four reasons we adopted Mac. One, we trusted the people who recommended Mac to us. Two, we hoped he would be a stabilizing and comforting companion for Bo. Three, when the day came when Bo would no longer be with us, Mac would be here to help us through our grief. And four, he had a sweet, sweet spirit about him.

Mac and Bo accepted each other from the beginning. Although they were very different, they lived in harmony and even met each other's shortcomings.

When we left them at home alone, Mac eased Bo's anxiety by curling up on the couch with him and resting his head on Bo's back. Bo returned the favor when bad weather caused Mac's panic attacks. Bo had learned not to be afraid of storms, so when he curled up to sleep through them, Mac curled up with him. They lay side by side through good times and bad.

Bo also encouraged Mac to get in the car. He eagerly jumped in first and claimed his spot, but Mac wouldn't get in at all. The minute we opened the car door, Mac lay down, rolled over on his back, and wouldn't budge. Like Superman, he could leap tall buildings in a single bound, but he couldn't get in the car by himself. I had to pick up his front feet, place them on the floorboard, then lift up his back end, and push him in. And every time I picked up his back end, he sat down in my hands.

In three years spent together, Mac and Bo never fought over food, toys, or who went first. They always waited their turn when being hooked to their leashes, or fed, or handed a toy. Mac always let Bo go to his food bowl first before going to his. If both of them wanted a ball, Mac deferred to Bo and let Bo have it. Mac seemed to understand that Bo needed the ball, while he did not.

At all times and in all ways, Mac and Bo were devoted to one another in brotherly love. They lived together in harmony, honored each other above themselves, and enjoyed the love of their master together. They defined unity and showed me that their special oneness with me was the bond that knit them together.

When we understand that our Master loves us individu-ally—totally apart from anyone else—and that He meets our needs, comforts us through the storms of life, and is faithful to be with us, our faith and trust in Him grows. We begin to love Him and want to spend more time with Him. And the closer we walk with the Master, the closer we walk with others in brotherly love.

> *Accept one another, then,*
> *just as Christ accepted you,*
> *in order to bring praise to God.*
>
> ROMANS 15:7 NIV

Heavenly Father, draw us into perfect unity with You so we can live in harmony with one another.

All of you be of one mind,
having compassion for one another;
love as brothers, be tenderhearted,
be courteous.

1 PETER 3:8

*Make every effort to keep
yourselves united in the spirit
binding yourselves together
with peace.*

EPHESIANS 4:2–3 NLT

A friend loves at all times.

PROVERBS 17:17

*A faithful friend
is the medicine of life.*

APOCRYPHA

17

Life and Death Decisions

Give me understanding, that
I may learn Your commandments.

PSALM 119:73

Karen, Mac's foster mom, said, "There are two commands our dogs must obey: 'stay' and 'come.' I use whatever it takes to make sure they obey those two, because they can make a difference between life and death."

Her advice rattled in my brain the first time I let Mac run free in the woods.

For the first three months I had kept him on a leash every time we went outside the fence. I knew from his history he was prone to wander. But on this particular day, when the woods were quiet and no deer were in sight, I let Mac run free.

He stayed relatively close and came back to my side when called until we topped the hill and headed home. As soon as Mac recognized the backyard, he took off to find LuLu, his Doberman/Rottweiler playmate who lived down the road. Thankfully she led him home.

LuLu came inside our fence, but Mac bypassed the gate to check out the front yard, too. Then he followed our long driveway to the road. I could hear a car in the distance and hurried down the driveway.

Mac had crossed the road and was running alongside it. The driver slowed down to watch out for him. When she saw me with leash in hand, she stopped to allow Mac to cross the road to me.

I waved a thank you, grabbed Mac's harness, then his muzzle, and rapped his nose yelling, "Bad dog!"

Yes, Mac had been a bad dog, but while I hooked him to his leash I had the feeling that I hadn't handled the situation properly. Obviously I'd done a poor job of teaching Mac to stay and come on command. When I returned to the house I e-mailed Karen about what had happened and asked her how I should have handled it. She said:

"When Mac comes to you or you catch him, please do not correct him. He'll be less willing to come next time if he knows when you get your hands on him he'll be reprimanded. Even if you'd like to string him up by his eyelashes, tell him how wonderful he is and give him a goodie. Make him really want to come back."

Her advice made perfect sense. I wouldn't want to return to someone for a rap on the nose either, would you?

Learning to sit, stay, and come helped Bo deal with his separation anxiety, and we hoped those same commands would control Mac's yearn to run. He had just proven that obedience to my commands could mean the difference between life and death. If he wanted to make it home safely, he needed to follow my rules and trust that I would work all things for his good because I knew what was best for them.

In the same way, I need to defer to God's will for my life and trust that He will work all things for my good because He knows what's best for me. As I pondered that point, I realized that those same commands to "stay" and "come" work well for both Mac and me.

When I say, "Stay," I mean stop, halt, or wait right where you are. When God tells me to "stay," He wants me to wait for Him and not run ahead of Him. He'll tell me where to go, what to do, and when the time is right.

When I say, "Come," I mean approach, advance, or draw near to me. Follow me. I know the way. I know the path I want you to follow, and I will lead you in safety. When my Master says, "Come, follow me," He means, " 'I know the plans I have for you . . . plans to prosper you and not to harm you, plans to give you hope and a future' " (Jeremiah 29:11 NIV).

When my dogs are obedient to my commands, they are rewarded with goodies.

And if I am obedient to my Master's commands, one day I will hear, " 'Come, you blessed of My Father, inherit the kingdom prepared for you from the foundation of the world' " (Matthew 25:34).

Heavenly Father, help me to understand Your commands that I might walk in obedience.

*"Whoever desires to come after Me,
let him deny himself, and
take up his cross, and follow Me."*

MARK 8:34

*Trust in the LORD with all your heart
and lean not on your own understanding;
in all your ways acknowledge him,
and he will make your paths straight.*

PROVERBS 3:5–6 NIV

LuLu the Rescue

LuLu was a cute little Doberman/Rottweiler puppy with floppy ears when her owners brought her to the country, let her out, and drove off. Lucky for LuLu, she landed in my neighborhood. A friend down the road adopted her, had her spayed, and gave her the love that all of us crave from our Master.

LuLu stayed with us once when her mom went out of town, and she went back home every day to see if her mom was back yet. The day her mom called to say, "I'm back," LuLu stayed home for days without coming to see me.

Then one morning as Bo and I walked in the woods, I heard LuLu's thundering paws rushing up behind me. When I turned around, she stopped suddenly and flung herself at my feet. She leaned against my legs, looked up at me for a chest rub, then slid to the forest floor with her tender tummy bared in total submission.

How long has it been since you offered your whole heart to your Master in total submission?

18

A Leash and a Prayer

*"Therefore you shall keep the commandments
of the LORD your God, to walk in His ways and to fear Him."*

DEUTERONOMY 8:6

My dogs love walking attached to their leashes. They joyfully submit to my control over them to go walking with me. The instant they hear the clasp hit the leash housing, Mac starts jumping up and down, and Bo throws his head back and howls. They wiggle so much I can't get a firm grasp on their collar rings, so they must sit and stay before I hook them up.

One of the benefits of walking them is that their excitement gives me the opportunity to reinforce their obedience to my commands and to conform them to the standard of behavior I've set for them. It's not enough for them to just sit. They must also stay until they are bound to me with a tether of love that enables me to lead, guide, and protect them as we walk together.

Walking on a leash makes them more aware of the world around them and gives them more opportunities to learn appropriate behavior in a variety of circumstances. For instance, when I hear or see a car coming, a simple tug and the word "stay" stops them wherever they are and allows me to shorten the leash, come alongside of them, and stand between them and the road to protect them. It allows me to protect them from people with rocks and sticks. It allows me to protect cats, kids on bikes, and other characters from being chased. And a swift yank of the leash keeps Mac from eating or rolling in the latest road kill.

Lengthening the leash gives them the freedom to run ahead, while shortening the leash encourages them to walk beside me. And when I continue to walk while Bo stops to smells the flowers or Mac stops to sniff out a deer crossing, a tug of the leash says, "Come, follow me."

In the same way, prayer—like a leash—is the lifeline of communication that God uses to lead, guide, and protect us and bring us into obedience. Prayer binds us to the Master to conform us to His good and perfect will. No wonder God wants us to pray without ceasing. We need to practice obedience as much as Mac and Bo do.

The more I talk to my Master and stay connected to Him through prayer, the more He can teach me, instruct me in the things He wants me to know, and even prepare me for coming events that I know nothing about. When I'm in close contact with the Lord, I listen more closely for His voice. I know when He draws me closer to protect me or to show me His love. I know when He allows me more freedom to roam and when He wants to comfort me or guide me past the obstacles in my life.

While Mac continues to run ahead of me and requires more yanks on his leash to conform him to my will, I've noticed that Bo wants to walk beside me more and more as he ages. I've discovered that's true in my life, too. The older I grow, the more I humble myself to the sovereignty of God and the more I want to walk with Him instead of running ahead of Him. Have you discovered that too?

Now when I walk the dogs, I'm more aware that my Master wants me to walk with Him.

When I tug on Mac's leash to keep him from veering off our path, I ask God to show me the path He wants me to walk.

When I protect my dogs from traffic, I thank God for protecting me.

And when I bring my dogs to my side, proudly claim them as my own, and introduce them to others, I'm reminded that God claims me as His own and loves me even more than I love my dogs.

Heavenly Father, teach me Your way, O Lord, that I might walk in obedience to Your commands.

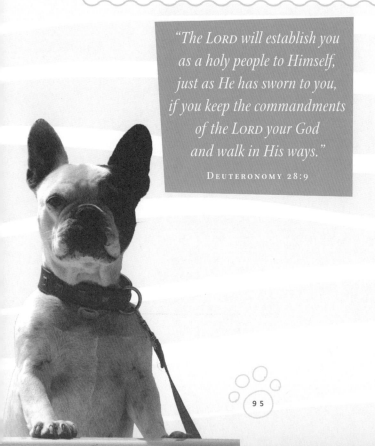

"The LORD will establish you as a holy people to Himself, just as He has sworn to you, if you keep the commandments of the LORD your God and walk in His ways."

DEUTERONOMY 28:9

Fetch

Because you love him, walk your dog on a retractable leash. You'll both enjoy more freedom. Leash sizes are based on your dog's weight.

PRAYER—LIKE A LEASH—IS THE LIFELINE OF COMMUNICATION GOD USES TO LEAD, GUIDE, AND PROTECT US AND BRING US INTO OBEDIENCE.

19

Wild Goose Chase

I will search for the lost and bring back the strays.
I will bind up the injured and strengthen the weak.

EZEKIEL 34:16 NIV

Mac had been with us for five months when we moved from the country to the lake. During that time he had only been allowed to run free once, and that almost ended in disaster. So even on our long walks in the woods when Bo ran free, Mac walked on a leash. At the lake we hadn't fenced the yard yet, so every day we walked both dogs on leashes along the bluff and took them down to the lake, where Bo roamed freely while Mac swam. Although Bo preferred not to get his feet wet, Mac loved the water so we impaled his retractable leash on a wrought iron stake driven into the ground at the water's edge. That way we could let him swim while we worked in the yard. With a twenty-six-foot range in any direction, Mac didn't seem to mind being tethered.

Because our property was in a quiet cove, we began letting Mac off the leash to swim while we cleaned up the trash that floated in every day. He had swum freely and stayed close to us several times before the first gaggle of geese he'd ever seen flew into the cove and swam toward him. Mac stood up on his hind legs in the water and uttered a strange guttural language I hadn't heard before. The geese must have understood because they stood up on the water, flapped their wings, and honked. Then with a powerful push of his back legs, Mac sprang toward the geese, and the race was on.

"Mac, stay!" I commanded.

"Mac, come!"

But he never heard my voice.

His hunting instincts consumed his thoughts. He went on full point, but instead of holding perfectly still, his feet and legs paddled with determined "get the geese" concentration. The geese split into two groups, but that didn't bother Mac. He shifted his attention to the slower group and paddled harder. When Mac started closing the gap, father goose fell in behind them and waited for Mac to catch up while the group paddled to safety. He teased Mac with his close proximity, then sped up again. And Mac paddled all the harder as father goose led him on a wild goose chase.

With no sign that Mac would give up, I feared he would drown from exhaustion. He had already swum a hundred yards and headed out to the big lake. We would have to go get him. My husband went back to the house to get the truck. He drove down the bluff far enough to get ahead of Mac and walked out on a neighbor's dock while I watched from the cove.

"Mac!" he called.

When Mac heard his name, he turned his head toward Earl's voice and started swimming in his direction. He swam alongside the dock all the way to the bank where Earl helped him out of the water and hooked him up to his leash.

With legs trembling from exhaustion, Mac followed Earl to the truck for the ride home.

As Bo and I walked back up the hill to the house, I thanked God for His faithfulness to take care of Mac. That's when He reminded me, *Earl left you and Bo to find Mac just like I left the ninety-nine to find you.* He recalled for me Matthew 18:12–13: " 'If a man has a hundred sheep, and one of them goes astray, does he not leave the ninety-nine and go to the mountains to seek the one that is straying? And if he should find it, . . . he rejoices more over that sheep than over the ninety-nine that did not go astray.'"

We were happy to have Mac back for sure. But I was even happier that God found me when I once wandered off on my own wild goose chase.

Have you ever done that? Are you wandering right now? It's hard to hear God's voice in the midst of disobedience, but when you come to the end of your strength like Mac did, you'll be relieved to know that God left the ninety-nine to find you and bring you back into the safety of His fold.

Mac is safe at home because he responded to his master's voice. I hope you will too.

Father, You said, "there will be more joy in heaven over one sinner who repents than over ninety-nine just persons who need no repentance" (Luke 15:7). Father, turn our hearts to You so the rejoicing can begin.

*If anyone among you wanders
from the truth, and someone turns him back,
let him know that he who turns a sinner from the error
of his way will save a soul from death
and cover a multitude of sins.*

JAMES 5:19–20

THE DISPOSITION OF NOBLE DOGS
IS TO BE GENTLE WITH PEOPLE
THEY KNOW AND THE OPPOSITE
WITH THOSE THEY DON'T KNOW. . . .
HOW, THEN, CAN THE DOG BE ANYTHING
OTHER THAN A LOVER OF LEARNING
SINCE IT DEFINES WHAT'S ITS OWN
AND WHAT'S ALIEN.

PLATO

20

What Are You Chasing?

And you will seek Me and find Me,
when you search for Me with all your heart.

JEREMIAH 29:13

Mac had been outside for thirty minutes when Bo and I walked down the hill toward the lake to look for him. While Bo nosed around the yard, I sat down in the swing to visually scan the cove for Mac. But before I settled in, the loud rustling of leaves startled me. I looked up in time to see a two-hundred-pound doe thundering in my direction. Then quick as greased lightning, she sidestepped to miss me, sidestepped to miss Bo, and disappeared into the woods behind us.

I watched Bo's head snap to attention after she whizzed by him and instantly understood the motivation for the song "Grandma Got Run Over by a Reindeer." Life is indeed fleeting.

A few seconds later we learned what spooked her as Mac burst from the woods running as hard as he could and losing ground with every step. Then he, too, disappeared after her.

Proverbs 12:11 says, "He who chases fantasies lacks judgment" (NIV).

I don't know if dogs have fantasies or not, but Mac certainly lacked judgment when he chased that doe. If by some freak of nature he had caught up with her, he would have been pummeled to death by her hooves.

As I sat in the swing and waited for him to return, I thought about the foolish things I've pursued during my life: a higher tennis ranking, a better golf score, or anything that would keep me from cleaning house. Have you pursued foolish things too?

But what if we ran hard after God the way Mac ran hard after that doe?

What if we turned from the busyness of our lives and sought God's face instead of more facts about Him?

What if we sought His presence to just talk to Him instead of offering Him traditional, repetitive, or prewritten prayers?

What if we longed and yearned for a closer personal relationship with Him?

God answered all those "what ifs" in a letter to those exiled in Babylon. He said:

> For I know the thoughts that I think toward you, says
> the LORD, thoughts of peace and not of evil, to give you a
> future and a hope. Then you will call upon Me and go and
> pray to Me, and I will listen to you. And you will seek Me
> and find Me, when you search for Me with all your heart.
> I will be found by you, says the LORD, and I will bring you
> back from your captivity.
>
> JEREMIAH 29:11–14

Wow! God has plans for us. He wants us to stop running hard after our fantasies and start putting our heart filled efforts into pursuing Him. He wants to prosper us and fill us with hope. He wants to draw us closer and hear our prayers.

Where are you in your relationship with God? Are you closer today than you were yesterday, or are you still chasing your fantasies? Wherever you are, God wants you closer.

Bo knows his master wants him closer. He jumped up into the swing and nestled in my lap while we waited for Mac to return. And while we waited, I remembered God's words in Jeremiah 31:3: " 'I have loved you with an everlasting love; Therefore with lovingkindness I have drawn you.' "

Bo and I waited another ten minutes before Mac reappeared with his tongue dragging the ground. He was exhausted, defeated, and weak from the chase. But he knew that he would regain his strength in the presence of his master. You will too.

Isn't it time to seek Him with your whole heart?

> *And you shall love the LORD*
> *your God with all your heart,*
> *with all your soul, with all your mind,*
> *and with all your strength.*
>
> MARK 12:30

Heavenly Father, thank You for loving us with an everlasting love. Turn us away from chasing our fantasies and lead us back to You.

21

I Ate the Whole Thing

"Is not life more important than food?"

MATTHEW 6:25 NIV

Mac doesn't think life is more important than food. Sometimes he doesn't think at all.

One Thanksgiving Day he reminded me of the problems of overeating when he chose to chow down on a feast of his own hunting. He caught and ate a groundhog. He ate the whole thing—from its nose to its rear toes—and he waddled home looking like he was nine months pregnant.

Friday afternoon, he started throwing up. Then he became dehydrated. After an emergency visit to the vet for X-rays and a liter of injected fluids, my husband and I spent three days pushing prescriptions down one end and suppositories up the other to quell his nausea and gastroenteritis.

By Monday morning he still refused food and had only been allowed to drink the water from two melted ice cubes during his trips to the water bowl. Blood work and more X-rays revealed acute pancreatitis, which is sometimes fatal and can lead to further complications unless we restrict his current lifestyle of chasing critters around the cove. You see, Mac doesn't know when to stop eating, but we do.

Why then do we continue to eat until we're more stuffed than a Thanksgiving turkey?

If it's because "everything looks so good," we can expect to suffer the consequences like Mac did. And if we survive those, we can expect to have to rely on lifestyle changes to reduce our high blood pressure, high blood sugar, and high cholesterol.

Mac has been put on restriction for life because he doesn't have the sense to discipline himself. But God gave us the good sense to discipline ourselves. If we fail to do so, He will do it for us because "the LORD disciplines those He loves" (Proverbs 3:12 NIV). And He loves us more than we love ourselves.

Celebrations throughout the year are occasions for big family dinners, bountiful buffets, and sweet smelling smorgasbords to tempt us with foods that fatten our figures, sour our stomachs, and cause our intestines to tumble.

Afterward, we sing the "I can't believe I ate the whole thing" blues.

But you know what? It doesn't have to be that way.

We don't have to eat the whole thing. We don't have to eat like a scavenger at a banquet. We don't have to eat as if we don't trust that God will provide our next meal.

Now even Mac knows that life is more important than food. Surely we do too.

So the next time we belly up to the buffet, let's remember Mac's misery, and back away before we do ourselves bodily harm. Let's ask those around us to help us eat responsibly and give them permission to take away our forks.

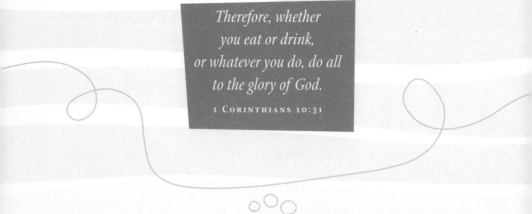

Therefore, whether you eat or drink, or whatever you do, do all to the glory of God.

1 CORINTHIANS 10:31

Father, lead us not into temptation but deliver us from the evil of overeating. Lead us from the desire to taste every bite on the buffet to savoring a life of discipline and good health.

THE FOOL THAT EATS
TILL HE IS SICK MUST FAST
TILL HE IS WELL.
WALTER THORNBURY

I SAW FEW DIE OF HUNGER;
OF EATING, A HUNDRED THOUSAND.
BENJAMIN FRANKLIN

THEY HAVE DIGGED THEIR GRAVE
WITH THEIR TEETH.
THOMAS ADAMS

22

Security You Can Count On

The Lord shall preserve you from all evil;
He shall preserve your soul.
The Lord shall preserve your going out and your coming in
From this time forth, and even forevermore.

PSALM 121:7–8

When we moved to the lake, Mac thought it was his responsibility to keep the cove safe from all the other animals. Every time we let him out the back door, he bounded down the hill to scour the shoreline and surrounding hills to chase away all intruders. He didn't understand that it was our responsibility to keep him safe instead.

We needed some boundaries to control his coming and going, so we fenced in a portion of the backyard. We wanted to protect him from potentially rabid animals like the family of foxes and a colony of raccoons roaming the neighborhood.

When the chain-link fence was installed, my husband and I stood on the back deck watching Mac examine every inch of his new boundaries. He didn't like the fence. It restricted his freedom. So he nosed the bottom links looking for a way out.

"That reminds me of Sadie," I said.

Sadie was a former neighbor's blue tick hound who came to our house every morning for a chest rub. If she saw me at the kitchen window, she crawled under our fence, ran up on the deck, and knocked on the door with her tail. After she received her chest rub, she ran back to the fence, put her shoulder to the ground, and slid back out the way she came in.

Suddenly Mac found a gap between the ground and the bottom of the fence. Just like Sadie, he lowered his right shoulder, turned sideways, and slid under the fence. He ran straight to the lake without looking back.

"That's probably how he got loose in Atlanta," Earl said. "I'll bet he slipped under the fence while his folks were at work."

"Well, that's not going to happen here," I vowed.

Since Mac had just shown us how he could escape, I spent the next hour blocking his escape route and examining the fence for other weak areas. Then I gathered a dozen half-inch-thick wrought iron stakes, wove them through the bottom links of the fence, and pounded them into the ground with a sledge hammer.

"There. That ought to hold him."

On the way back to the house I thanked God for protecting me without fencing me in. I'm in His protective custody everywhere I go.

> He protects me day and night.
> He hides me in the shadow of His wings.
> He commands His angels concerning me.
> He guards my course, protects my way, and surrounds me
>   with songs of deliverance.
> He is my shield, my strength, my salvation; my rock, my
>   fortress, and my Savior who watches over my coming and
>   going both now and forevermore. So, whom shall I fear?

Do you know the security the Lord offers those who believe in Him? Unlike a chain-link fence, the Lord provides security we can count on.

Heavenly Father, You promised, "If [we] make the Most High [our] dwelling . . . then no harm will befall [us]" (Psalm 91:9–10 NIV). Thank You for Your faithfulness to protect us.

*He guards the paths
of the just and protects those
who are faithful to him.*

PROVERBS 2:8 NLT

*In the fear of the LORD
there is strong confidence,
and His children will have
a place of refuge.*

PROVERBS 14:26

23

A Powerful Cleansing Agent

*For we are to God the fragrance of Christ among those who
are being saved and among those who are perishing.*

2 CORINTHIANS 2:15

Only one thing smells worse than a dead skunk in the middle of the road,
and that's the lingering wake of a skunk-sprayed-in-the-face-dog flying through
the house. That's what happened to our first dog, Augie.

We didn't know he'd been squirted until we opened the door to let him in
on that freezing February day. Before we could collar him and usher him back
outside he had rolled on the couch, rubbed against the drapes, and rollicked in
the middle of our bed trying to get the smell off of him.

That's when we discovered that opening all the windows and turning
on the attic fan doesn't help in getting rid of the stench. Laundering or dry
cleaning fabrics does not remove the smell either. And tomato juice only turns
a white dog red.

I'd forgotten about that incident with Augie until the morning Mac got
skunked. He cornered one in the bottom of the cove and killed it, but not
before the skunk emptied its jets on Mac's face and chest.

That morning started like every other morning. Mac stood beside my bed
whining at dawn. I reached my hand out from under the covers, patted him on the
head, and hoped he would let me go back to sleep. After all, it was only 5:30 and
still dark outside. But he stuck his muzzle under my wrist and tossed my arm into

the air. Knowing he wasn't going to let me roll over, I got up to let him out.

After traipsing through the wet grass in the dark, I opened the back gate to let him run free for a few minutes. That was the only freedom we allowed him since he caught and ate the groundhog and nearly died. My husband had said, "He'll only be gone a few minutes because he knows breakfast is waiting for him." It sounded reasonable, and that theory actually worked until he met the skunk.

I heard him barking like he had something cornered. So I grabbed a flashlight, his leash, and a walking stick to use as a weapon if needed. My mission was to get whatever it was away from him before he ate it and got sick again.

By the time I walked down the hill, a pack of stray dogs had gathered around Mac and the skunk. Thankful that God had given me dominion over the animals, I raised my stick in the air and yelled, "Get out of here!"

I stood amazed as the whole pack of dogs ran up the hill, and I was thankful that they didn't turn on me and kill me. Then I turned my attention to Mac and the skunk.

"Come here, Mac," I said from fifteen feet away.

I showed him his leash. With a little more coaxing, he left the skunk, let me hook him up, and looked back only once before climbing the hill to the house with me.

From past experience I knew what didn't work to get the skunk smell out, so while Mac stayed outside I logged onto the Internet to find something that did work. The word "explosive" caught my eye—an "explosive" concoction of hydrogen peroxide, baking soda, and dishwashing detergent added to a gallon of water.

"That ought to do the trick."

The directions said, "The recipe must be mixed up and used quickly. It loses its effectiveness within about an hour, and it will explode if it's kept in a covered container."

I figured if it was that powerful, it was just what I needed, because Mac had a powerful stink about him.

Mac stayed on the back deck while I waited until 6:30 to call a neighbor and borrow a box of baking soda. Then with all ingredients in hand, I mixed half a batch of this explosive concoction in a large glass bowl and carried it gingerly to the back door and down the deck steps.

Mac stood still while I removed his collar, tossed it into the bowl, and then soaked every square inch of his body with a saturated sponge. As I sponged across his muzzle, between his eyes, and around his mouth I thought about the powerful cleansing agent it took to cleanse me of my sin. And I wondered if I had ever left the kind of a stench in God's nostrils that Mac had burned in mine.

Softly I began to sing the old hymn as I squeezed the sponge into Mac's coat. "What can wash away my sin? Nothing but the blood of Jesus. What can make me whole again? Nothing but the blood of Jesus."

The smell began to dissipate as each squeeze of the sponge sent rivulets of the power cleaner deep into his coat. "Oh! Precious is the flow That makes me white as snow; No other fount I know, Nothing but the blood of Jesus" ("Nothing but the Blood" by Robert Lowry).

When Mac had soaked for five minutes, I rinsed and toweled him dry. His white legs and chest shone brighter than ever. The rest of his muted brown coat turned deep chocolate. And the skunk smell was gone.

I walked Mac up the steps and into the house knowing that since our deep cleansing, we'd both leave a better fragrance in our wake.

Heavenly Father, "thanks be to God who always leads us in triumph in Christ, and through us diffuses the fragrance of His knowledge in every place" (2 Corinthians 2:14).

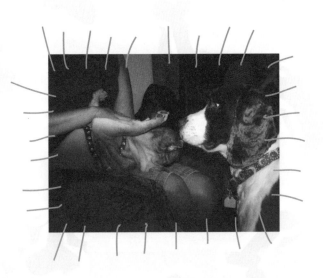

Fetch

If your pet meets a skunk, mix the following ingredients:

$\frac{1}{4}$ CUP BAKING SODA

1 TABLESPOON DISHWASHING LIQUID

1 BOTTLE HYDROGEN PEROXIDE

1 GALLON WATER

Sponge into your pet's coat. Rinse with water after five minutes. Warning: explosive! Do not cover. Pour out unused portion.

INTO THE PRESENCE, FLATTENING WHILE I CRAWL—
FROM HEAD TO TAIL, I DO CONFESS IT ALL.
MINE WAS THE FAULT—DEAL ME THE STRIPES—BUT SPARE
THE POINTED FINGER WHICH I CANNOT BEAR!
THE DREADFUL TONE IN WHICH MY NAME IS NAMED,
THAT SEND ME 'NEATH THE SOFA-FRILL ASHAMED!
(YET TO BE NEAR THEE I WOULD FACE THE WOE.)
IF THOU REJECT ME, WHITHER SHALL I GO?

FROM "SUPPLICATION OF
THE BLACK ABERDEEN"
BY RUDYARD KIPLING

23

The Gate Is Closing

*"Strive to enter through the narrow gate, for many,
I say to you, will seek to enter and will not be able."*

LUKE 13:24

A couple of weeks after Mac got used to being fenced in, I began letting him run for a few minutes before breakfast. It was the only free run he was allowed. I knew he wouldn't be gone longer than five minutes. He didn't want to miss a meal. But one morning Mac scoured the shoreline of the cove while I stood at the back gate calling him.

"Mac? Come. Here, Mac."

He bounded halfway up the hill and stopped.

"Good boy, Mac. Come on. Let's go to the house," I said.

He looked at me, then looked back at the lake. I didn't know whether he'd rather feed his belly or his instinct to hunt, but I hadn't won him over yet, so I softened my voice.

"Mac, come on, buddy."

He took another step in my direction, then he looked back at the lake again.

While he was still trying to decide whether to follow my call or to follow the call of the wild, I spoke his name once more.

"Come on, Mac," I said. "The gate is closing."

His eyes widened as he watched my hand pull the gate toward me. Then with a sudden burst of energy, Mac sprinted inside before being completely shut out.

As we walked to the house I thought, *we humans are just like Mac.* We stand on the edge of eternity not knowing when that narrow gate will close, but one thing we know for sure. The gate will close. So today we have to make the same decision Mac had to make. Will we follow the Good Master home or will we follow the ways of the world?

> Jesus said,
>
> "Strive to enter through the narrow gate, for many, I say to you, will seek to enter and will not be able. When once the Master of the house has risen and shut the door, and you begin to stand outside and knock at the door, saying, Lord, Lord, open for us, and He will answer and say to you, I do not know you, where you are from. . . . There will be weeping and gnashing of teeth, when you see Abraham and Isaac and Jacob and all the prophets in the kingdom of God, and yourselves thrust out."
>
> LUKE 13:24–25, 28

Today while the gate is still open, Jesus urges us, "Come, follow Me." But one day Jesus will step out on a cloud and call His followers to the home He has prepared for us. People will come from all points of the globe to feast in the kingdom of God. Will you be among them? Will you have made the only decision that matters during your life here on earth?

The gate is closing now. Do you feel the urgency for deciding? Mac did. He sprinted to be inside the gate with his master. How will you respond?

Heavenly Father, You said that You don't want anyone to perish. Fill us with the urgency to respond to Your call so we will not have to face Your judgment. Father, impress upon us the urgency to follow Your Son now, so we can enjoy an eternal life of rejoicing in Your presence.

Multitudes, multitudes
in the valley of decision!
For the day of the LORD
is near in the valley of decision.

JOEL 3:14

NOT TO DECIDE IS TO DECIDE.

ANONYMOUS

GOD OFFERS
TO EVERY MIND ITS CHOICE
BETWEEN TRUTH AND REPOSE.

EMERSON

THE DOOR MUST EITHER
BE SHUT OR BE OPEN.

GOLDSMITH

DELIBERATE AS OFTEN AS YOU PLEASE,
BUT WHEN YOU DECIDE IT IS ONCE FOR ALL.

PUBLILIUS SYRUS

25

Pay Careful Attention

We must pay more careful attention,
therefore, to what we have heard,
so that we do not drift away.

HEBREWS 2:1 NIV

The dogs and I returned from our evening canoe ride.

I held onto the side of the dock and said, "Okay, guys. Get out."

Bo stared at me, panting, with that dumb "who, me?" look on his face that is common to Springers. He loves canoeing. He's always the first one in and the last one to get out, while Mac just jumps joyously from one event to the next with eager anticipation of what life has to offer. But at that moment, Mac's attention riveted on a floating leaf.

"Get out," I repeated.

Both ignored my second command, too. They like to be where I am, and since I was still in the canoe, they were going to stay put. Realizing that, I stepped out of the canoe and tied it to a cleat on the dock. Mac followed me.

The powerful push of his back legs catapulted the canoe out of my reach, yanked the rope out of my hand, and set Bo adrift to the far side of the cove.

If Bo had paid attention and jumped out when I told him, he would have been safe with me on the dock instead of drifting along, tossed by every wave.

The canoe finally floated to the opposite shore. I walked around to the other side of the cove, waded into the water, and stepped back into the canoe.

As I paddled back to the dock, I thought about the times I've gotten in trouble because I didn't pay attention. Like Mac and Bo, I hear what I want to hear and ignore the rest. Do you do that?

And yet, the Good Master's directions to us are so simple. Listen and obey.

I need to be so attuned to God's voice that I'm listening for it before He speaks; because if I'm not listening, I might not hear it at all. And if I'm not careful, I could drift away just like Bo did.

So I must pay more careful attention, too, lest I become influenced by the prevailing wind of thought, or the next new theory about God, or someone else trying to push me in another direction. How about you? Isn't it time we paid attention?

Jesus Christ, the Son of God, will perfect our faith if we don't drift away from Him.

Heavenly Father, soften our hearts to pay attention, so that when we hear Your voice, we might respond in obedience and not drift away.

Teach me Your way, O LORD;
I will walk in Your truth.

PSALM 86:11

26

Too Soon to Quit

There is a time for everything,
and a season for every activity under heaven:
a time to search and a time to give up.

ECCLESIASTES 3:1, 6 NIV

When Mac and Bo went to the vet for their yearly rabies shots and physicals, they were both declared physically fit. Even though Bo was thirteen years old, the vet said, "He ought to have two or three more good years left."

We left there overjoyed at the prospect of having deaf, emotionally challenged, one-eyed Bo around another few years. But three weeks later he started going downhill fast.

One day his back end collapsed as he tried to go up the stairs to the back deck. The next day he refused to walk his usual half mile. Then he started dragging his left foot and whimpering. X-rays at the vet's office revealed the jagged edges of osteoarthritis that had claimed 50 percent of his left femoral ball and 25 percent of the right one. He had been playing too rough with Mac, and now his pain was excruciating.

The vet said, "With the arthritis medicines and injections to cushion the hip socket, we've seen immediate results from dogs in worse shape."

With that encouragement we looked for immediate results for Bo too. But that didn't happen.

The first meds Bo took caused such stomach pain that he cried and panted heavily for five hours after the first tablet. So we experimented with other anti-inflammatories and painkillers while Bo continued to drag his foot and cry. I spent the entire week comforting him through the night and hoping the meds would kick in.

Other than his hips, Bo was in good health and still eating well, but we couldn't stand to see him suffer. We agonized over what to do. Should we keep searching for the right combination of medicines? Would he get any better? Would he ever have a decent quality of life again? Or was it time to put him down?

At what point do we say enough is enough?

So I prayed, *Lord, I don't know the number of his days, but You do. What should we do? He can't continue to suffer like this. Is it time to put him down?*

Finally my husband said, "Call the vet. You're going to have to take him in Monday."

So I made the appointment to have him put down.

The instant I hung up the phone, I began having second thoughts. Knowing that Bo was a "dead dog walking" was more than I could handle. We cried with Bo all weekend knowing we were going to lose him. The only way we could bear that burden was in knowing that we still had the option of starting Chondroprotec injections. They were the only things we hadn't tried.

I talked to God a lot during that time—I didn't want to put Bo down if there was any chance we could manage his pain and he could continue a decent quality of life.

After a weekend of anticipating Bo's death on Monday, grief had worn me to a frazzle. I needed to know that I was doing the right thing because I'd never forgive myself if I had him put down just because I couldn't stand to hear him cry.

I e-mailed Bo's foster mom, Christi, and told her the situation.

She said, "As long as he is eating well, that is always a sign that there is hope. Explore all options. Give Bo every chance. You will not be sorry for trying. . . . Allow the peace in your heart to guide you to the next step."

That peace came when I sat down to read a devotional booklet that I had not read in a while. God's answer to Bo's dilemma was right there in the title for that day: "Too Soon to Quit."

Immediately the burden lifted. With hope renewed, joy filled my heart. We would keep searching for the right combination of medicines and start him on the injections. If other dogs in worse shape had made amazing turnarounds, Bo could too.

Monday morning we took him to the vet to begin the Chondroprotec injections to provide more cushion in his hip sockets. We switched up his medicines to include Deramaxx to reduce inflammation; Tramadol to reduce pain; and sucralfate to lessen the stomach irritation from other meds. And through much prayer, wise counsel, and modern medicine, Bo began to feel better. His crying stopped. His breathing returned to normal. And he walked on all four feet, pain-free, happy, and even strutting again—albeit with an occasional limp. He learned to live with his disability, and we learned to live with it too.

From then on, the back deck steps were off limits to him; instead he came and went through the front door, which had only one step. Romping with Mac was vetoed, because Bo didn't know when to quit and always wound up getting hurt. And when he took a run to jump up on the couch, I cradled his back end in the crook of my arm to hoist him up pain free.

Because we turned to God for answers we didn't have, Bo's recovery amazed us. His pace quickened. He was out of pain, and the puppy in him returned.

God has the answers you're looking for, too. Whatever trial you're facing, God will most certainly see you through it. Seek His wisdom. He might be trying to tell you, "It's too soon to quit."

Heavenly Father, I'm so thankful that You chose not to reveal to us the number of our days. What a miserable lot we would be if we knew the time and date of our death. So thank You, Father, for each day You've given us to trust You with our decisions as we live this life one day at a time.

So teach us to number our days,
that we may gain a heart of wisdom.

PSALM 90:12

THERE IS SORROW ENOUGH IN THE NATURAL WAY
FROM MEN AND WOMEN TO FILL OUR DAY;
AND WHEN WE ARE CERTAIN OF SORROW IN STORE
WHY DO WE ALWAYS ARRANGE FOR MORE?
BROTHERS AND SISTERS, I BID YOU BEWARE
OF GIVING YOUR HEART TO A DOG TO TEAR.

RUDYARD KIPLING

THE POWER OF THE DOG

27

Wallowing

*If we confess our sins, He is faithful
and just to forgive us our sins and
to cleanse us from all unrighteousness.*

1 JOHN 1:9

Mac gets filthier on a five-minute free run than you or I could in a lifetime of scrubbing floors, cleaning out gutters, or doing yard work. His idea of fun is rolling in the greenest goose droppings, the latest catfish carcass to wash ashore, or the most maggot-infested rack of raccoon ribs he can find. Yes, he's really done all three.

He likes to drop to one side of his neck and get the goo caked behind his ear and in his collar. Then he slides to his upper leg, rolls over on his back, and smears it from shoulder to shoulder. He especially likes to drag a carcass to the hillside so he can turn over and slide headfirst through it like he's going down a sliding board on his back. That way he gets covered in slime from head to tail.

But no matter how many times Mac rolls in something disgusting, or what time of day it is, or how cold it is, he gets cleaned up when he comes home. We figure if he can slog through the mucky shoreline in midwinter, he can stand for a hosing with freezing water.

Why don't we just let him stay outside when he gets that nasty?

Because we want him with us. We enjoy his company. He is our friend, our companion, a well-loved member of our family. He lives in our house with us and abides by the same rules. We don't come in the house filthy, nasty, dirty, and neither does Mac. We won't let him in with the stench of death still on him.

We can expect a cleansing, too, when we've done wrong in God's eyes. Even though God wants us to come into His house and live with Him, He will not allow anybody or anything impure or dirty to enter His presence. But if we humble ourselves, confess our sins, and ask for His forgiveness with a sincere heart, God will cleanse us, forgive us, and purify us of all unrighteousness.

Mac knows when he needs to be cleansed. He stands humbly at the foot of the deck steps totally yielded to the consequences of his wallowing. Do you know when you need to be cleansed? Are you aware of when your preoccupation with self has caused you to wallow in self-pity, self-doubt, or self-loathing? Are you aware of when you've thought of yourself more highly than you ought, and you're self-centered, self-righteous, or self-serving?

God said that we've all sinned and fallen short of His glory. "We are all like an unclean thing, And all our righteousnesses are like filthy rags" (Isaiah 64:6).

But out of His great love for us, God cleans us up because He wants us with Him. He enjoys our company. He is our Good Master, and we are His friends, His companions, and well-loved members of His family. And because we are, we can humble ourselves before Him, confess our sins, and receive His forgiveness.

Mac is back in the house now after his cleansing. Are you ready to stand humbly at the feet of your Master and yield to the consequences of your wallowing?

Heavenly Father, have mercy on me, a sinner. Take away the guilt of my sin and purify me of all unrighteousness.

If You, LORD, should mark iniquities,
O LORD, who could stand?
But there is forgiveness with You,
that You may be feared.

PSALM 130:3-4

A DOG DIRTS THOSE MOST
WHOM HE LOVES BEST.

SWIFT

I TALK TO HIM WHEN I'M LONESOME LIKE,
AND I'M SURE HE UNDERSTANDS.
WHEN HE LOOKS AT ME SO ATTENTIVELY,
AND GENTLY LICKS MY HANDS;
THEN HE RUBS HIS NOSE
ON MY TAILORED CLOTHES,
BUT I NEVER SAY NAUGHT THREAT,
FOR THE GOOD LORD KNOWS
I CAN BUY MORE CLOTHES,
BUT NEVER A FRIEND LIKE THAT!

W. DAYTON WEDGEFARTH

28

Heart and Mouth Disease

Not what goes into the mouth defiles a man;
but what comes out of the mouth, this defiles a man.

MATTHEW 15:11

Have you ever seen a den wall decorated with the heads of animals you wished were still roaming free in the woods somewhere?

It's as if the hunter is saying, "Look what I bagged."

Mac, a sporting dog, has his kills, too, but his trophy wall wouldn't include the magnificent heads of deer, elk, or moose. If we mounted Mac's trophies, you'd see small game like a groundhog, possum, and skunk. You'd also see a catfish he caught, brought to shore, and held down with his foot to keep it from flopping.

Mac continues the thrill of the hunt even when he's limited to the fenced yard. With the patience of the most seasoned deer hunter, he starts on the deck sniffing the air to catch wind of smaller game, then pokes his head through the rails to look for movement in the grass. Once he spots the game, he bounds down the steps for the chase.

He's caught a rabbit and several chipmunks making a run for the fence, grabbed blue tail lizards off the side of the house, and snatched birds right out of the air. On a slow day Mac hunts worms and bugs. He noses the ground, diligently separating the blades of grass and finds grub worms that even the birds can't locate.

Based on Mac's hunting record, you might think that he is a vicious animal. But if you saw him play with small children, you would see his soft mouth and gentle heart. You see, it's not what goes into his mouth that matters, it's what comes out; and what comes out of his mouth is based on what's in his heart.

It was hard for me to understand how Mac could ruthlessly run down some poor critter and kill it then run back home to be a lap dog, lounging lovingly all over me, until I realized that we humans are just like him. We have killer mouths too. The things we say can hurt others as surely as Mac's vicious chomp.

We speak kindly to people's faces and talk about them behind their backs. We take every opportunity to tell a story that makes someone look foolish, and we don't hesitate to poke fun at each other. It's all for sport, right? A jab here, a put-down there, and a little clever repartee tossed around in good fun. Nothing wrong with that, right? Our wisecracks, barbs, and zingers don't hurt anybody's feelings. They know we're just funning them, don't they?

But sometimes those comments dig deeper than we intended. We can tell by someone's changed expression that we've gone too far, so we apologize.

"I'm sorry. I didn't mean to hurt your feelings."

"Then why did you say it?" they ask.

Good question. Why do we utter those careless words?

Jesus asked a more pointed question: " 'Why do you think evil in your hearts?' " (Matthew 9:4).

Evil thoughts? That's not what is in our hearts, is it? And yet our own mouths condemn us, and our own lips testify against us (Job 15:6).

James, the half brother of Jesus, chastises us: "Out of the same mouth proceed blessing and cursing. My brethren, these things ought not to be so" (James 3:10).

He's right. If our words reflect our heart's thoughts, we need open heart surgery to replace those thoughts with those that are pleasing to God. We need to think about "whatever is true, whatever is noble, whatever is right, whatever is pure, whatever is lovely, whatever is admirable . . . anything [that] is excellent or praiseworthy" (Philippians 4:8 NIV).

So let's build others up instead of tearing them down and make sure our words benefit those who listen (Ephesians 4:29 NIV). Let's resolve that our mouths will not sin. And let's stop running others down with careless words like Mac runs down a rabbit.

> "Out of the overflow of the heart the mouth speaks. . . .
> Men will have to give account on the day of judgment
> for every careless word they have spoken.
> For by your words you will be acquitted,
> and by your words you will be condemned."
>
> MATTHEW 12:34, 36–37 NIV

Heavenly Father, "Set a guard, O LORD, over my mouth; Keep watch over the door of my lips" (Psalm 141:3) so that the words of my mouth and the meditation of my heart may be pleasing in Your sight (Psalm 19:14).

*Singing psalms and hymns
and spiritual songs
among yourselves, and making music
to the Lord in your hearts.*

EPHESIANS 5:19 NLT

THE HEART OF ANY MATTER
IS A MATTER OF THE HEART.

UNKNOWN

FOR ATTRACTIVE LIPS,
SPEAK WORDS OF KINDNESS. . . .
PEOPLE, EVEN MORE THAN THINGS,
HAVE TO BE RESTORED, RENEWED,
REVIVED, RECLAIMED, AND REDEEMED.
NEVER THROW OUT ANYONE.

AUDREY HEPBURN

FIERCE IN THE WOODS.
GENTLE IN THE HOME.

MARTIAL

29

Do Dogs Go to Heaven?

Yea, though I walk through the valley of the shadow of death
I will fear no evil for Thou art with me.

PSALM 23:4 KJV

As a dog lover, you've probably had to have one of your beloved pets put to sleep. We have too. Our first dog, Augie, a pointer, was fourteen when our vet had to put him down. I made my husband take him, because emotionally I couldn't handle it. But Earl had a hard time dealing with it too. He came back from that experience saying, "I can't do that again. If it's got to be done, you are going to have to do it."

From then on, the responsibility for easing the passing of our dogs fell squarely on my shoulders. Each one of our beloved pets gave me too much joy to abandon them to the vet to die alone; so each one died in my arms knowing they were loved, and each one received a proper burial in a place of honor in one of my gardens.

I've been asked many times, "Do dogs go to heaven when they die?"

The simple answer is, I don't know. That's one of the mysteries God chose not to reveal to us in His Word. But He did reveal to us that heaven is a real place, and people who believe in His Son will inherit eternal life and go to heaven when they die.

Jesus said, "In My Father's house are many mansions; if it were not so, I would have told you. I go to prepare a place for you. And if I go and prepare a place for you, I will come again and receive you to Myself; that where I am, there you may be also" (John 14:2–3).

Today Jesus sits in heaven at the right hand of God the Father waiting to call us home. When the day comes that we enter into the other side of eternity, we'll know if our dogs are romping and playing in heaven. Until then, I hope they are. We just buried Bo under a dogwood tree in the backyard.

An undiagnosed problem caused a slow-moving but full-body paralysis one night. And just as Jesus promised me, "I will never leave you or forsake you," I never left Bo's side. I slept with him all night, called a mobile vet to come out early the next morning, and held him as he breathed his last.

While I don't know if Bo is romping and playing in heaven with all my other dogs, I do know that God has promised to comfort me in my grief and wipe every tear from my eyes. I know that He promised to make all things new one day. And I know that all creation waits to be liberated from the bondage of decay and brought into the glorious freedom of the children of God.

And there is one more thing I know. I know that Bo has eternal life, because his spirit lives on in my heart.

> *In His hand is the life of every creature*
> *and the breath of all mankind.*
>
> **JOB 12:10 NIV**

Heavenly Father, in Your great mercy comfort those who grieve the loss of their beloved friends.

He will swallow up death forever,
And the Lord GOD will wipe away
tears from all faces.

ISAIAH 25:8

HEAVEN GOES BY FAVOR.
IF IT WENT BY MERIT, YOU WOULD STAY OUT
AND YOUR DOG WOULD GO IN.

MARK TWAIN

You think dogs
will not be in heaven?
I tell you, they will be there
long before any of us.

Robert Lewis Stevenson

If I have any beliefs
about immortality,
it is that certain dogs
I have known will
go to heaven, and very,
very few persons.

James Thurber

144

WHEN IS THE RIGHT TIME?
YOU WILL KNOW. YOU WILL LOOK
AT THAT PRECIOUS FACE AT SOME POINT
AND KNOW THAT THE KINDEST THING
YOU CAN DO IS RELEASE HIM.

CHRISTI COOPER

BO WAS FAITHFUL TO ME
TO THE LAST BEAT OF HIS HEART.
I HOPE I WAS WORTHY
OF HIS DEVOTION.

LINDA HULTIN WINN

30

A New Day

*Weeping may endure for a night,
but joy comes in the morning.*

PSALM 30:5

With a summer of drought and Bo's illness, the dogs and I had not gone canoeing or kayaking at all. Our dock had been out of water all summer due to lack of rain. Even the backs of docks on deep water rested on the shore. So a month after Bo's death, Mac and I launched the canoe for the first time all summer. We put in at the neighborhood boat ramp and looked forward to a time of renewal, restoration, and moving on.

Once we were underway, Mac immediately moved to the front of the canoe to get the first look at each leaf that floated by. It was good to see the wag of his tail leading the way to new adventures of our own. Mac enjoyed being top dog.

A slight breeze, blue sky, and water slapping against the hull refreshed my spirit. We rounded point nine passing close to the shore. I looked for fish hiding under the rock shelves, and Mac leaned over the gunnels to examine old tree stumps with roots spread out like an octopus hugging the lake bottom.

Ten minutes later, we reached our neighbor's dock. He said we could use it for a while. As I tied up to a cleat, I noticed water in back of the canoe and couldn't remember enough splashing or dripping to accumulate that much. I thought the plug might be worn out, so Pete, the neighborhood mariner, came over to take a look.

We turned the canoe around and pulled the transom up on the shore. Pete examined the plug then put it back in.

A minute later he said, "It's not the plug. You've got a leak in the boat."

He pointed to small ripples where the hull met the transom. "Look right here."

"Yep. I'll have to take it out of the water. Can we make it back around the point?"

"Yeah, but stay close to the shore. I'll call Earl and tell him to meet you at the ramp."

Mac jumped back in the canoe, and we shoved off. I prayed, *Lord please don't let the water pressure cause a leak big enough to sink us.*

Mac had his life jacket on, and I put mine back on.

As we rounded the point I prayed, "Let me not sink, let me be delivered from...out of the deep waters" (Psalm 69:14 NKJV)

Mac wasn't worried about sinking, and after praying, I wasn't either.

Then, with the ramp in full view, we could see Earl in the distance. He already had the trailer in the water waiting to receive our disabled canoe. So our first boating adventure of the summer ended with a leak in the stern and a limp into port.

After Earl pulled the canoe onto the trailer and out of the water, he examined the leak, poking and prodding with his finger until the fiberglass gave way to reveal a one-inch gaping hole that most certainly would have sunk us had it given way. We ended our journey knowing that a season of our lives had come to an end.

Looking back, we've had good times in that old canoe, but now that it's in dry dock to have all her dings and scrapes repaired, I've decided to sell it. That season of our lives has ended, and a new one is beginning to bud.

I'm content walking along the lakeshore with Mac. He swims and walks a few steps, then looks up at me to be sure I'm still there. His docked tail wagging in the water spins like a small propeller and creates ripples of joy as we move on to new adventures and God's promise of a new day coming.

Heavenly Father, thank You for bringing us safely home. We look forward to a new day with You.

He leads me beside the still waters.
He restores my soul.
PSALM 23:2–3

Dogs Grieve Too

Mac misses his pack brother. He sticks to me like Velcro. Even when I open the gate for him, he does his business and runs right back. I call him "Mama's Boy." Earl calls him "Sissy Boy." Either way, we're both glad we have Mac to hug.

A New Trick

When a neighbor asked me to do latrine duty for their cat while they were away, I decided to take Mac with me and use that time to teach him how to jump into the car. The new-trick training was harder on me that it was on Mac.

The first three days, the only way I could get him in the car was to play follow the leader. I entered from the passenger side, crawled over the console, and called Mac to me. After five minutes of begging and coaxing, he gingerly stepped into the car.

On the fourth day, I coaxed him from the passenger side. He jumped in after a minute or so. On the fifth day, I stood beside him on the passenger side and said, "Okay, Mac. Jump in."

And without hesitation, that old dog showed me his new trick.

"Ask, and it will be given to you;
seek, and you will find; knock,
and it will be opened to you.
For everyone who asks receives,
and he who seeks finds,
and to him who knocks
it will be opened."

LUKE 11:9–10

IN SEARCH OF
THE GOOD MASTER

Consider Adoption Your First Option

Over a three year period, Christi Cooper, an obedience instructor, fostered and trained forty-five rescue dogs in her home. Because of her love and devotion to help the helpless, Bo, my special needs pup, thrived during his time with her.

Christi said, "We want the next home for our rescues to be their last, and we are committed to doing all we can to ensure they are on their way to being good companions when they are placed."

I hope her insight during a recent interview will prepare you to rescue your next dog.

HT: From your perspective, what is the main difference between getting a puppy and rescuing an adult dog?

CC: You have to earn trust with a rescue. Puppies take it for granted. A rescue dog takes nothing for granted. You have to prove to them that there is love outside of what they had the first time. And what is amazing is that no matter what happened before, they are willing to take that journey. It's a very different journey than the one the puppy will take. Bo was abandoned by someone he trusted; and that trust was not just compromised, it was seriously damaged.

HT: That's why Bo grabbed our heartstrings.

CC: Yeah, you start out where your heart aches for them, and you invest your love, time, and energy in these dogs, and when they do begin to trust us, the payoff is incredible. We somehow place a greater value on them and feel better about ourselves, because their trust is hard-earned.

HT: Then what is the key to working with a rescue dog versus a puppy?

CC: Small steps. You can shape a puppy's behavior quickly, but you have to shape a rescue in really small steps. And you may not shape the behavior you thought you were going to get, but chances are you'll get something much better when you treat him with respect.

HT: Knowing that rescues come with baggage and the give-and-take working with them requires, how would you advise someone who wants to adopt a rescue?

CC: I want them to be aware of the dog's background, talk with the one who fostered the dog, learn all they can about the dog's issues. Then they will know what to expect. For the person going on a Web site and looking at a particular dog, if that dog touches your heartstrings even in the slightest way, it's best you get that dog.

HT: That's a good tip.

CC: If a dog gets in your gut, there is a reason. So look at him. Ask questions about him. If someone is already coming to look at the dog, find out about the dog anyway. Get as much information as you can up front. The person coming to see the dog may not be the right home for that dog.

HT: So you try to match the rescues with the right people?

CC: Oh, yes. There were some folks who came for a particular dog, and I knew the match wasn't there. I had to say no. And that is not an easy thing to do because I don't like to reject anybody. But those dogs won my heart, and I had to do what was best for them.

HT: What advice do you have for the person who has taken a rescue dog home for the first time?

CC: I would advise them to let go of any pride or cockiness they might have about their ability to train a dog. You have to lose some of that attitude that says, "This is the way it's going to be," because you don't know all about that dog. Again, you have to work with them in small steps.

The dog will let you know, "I can go this way," or "I can't go that way. You have to find another way." You can't go into rescue and deal with each dog the same way.

HT: What is the goal of a rescue program?

CC: Every rescue dog needs a permanent and loving home to help him learn to trust again. We want to place the dog with a family that is worthy of the trust a rescue dog will learn to give them.

HT: What did you take away from your experience doing rescue work?

CC: I got to see the miracle of each dog learning to trust again. For some it was a tougher hill to climb than others. I will always have a great deal of respect for the dogs that shared my home. Each one of them owns a piece of my heart.

HT: How does working with a rescue with a trust issue change you on the inside?

CC: I have an overwhelming gratitude to God for the dogs that were brought to me and for the two that stayed. The ones that went on to loving homes were the homes meant for them. I was just the one who transitioned them from the life they had to the life they came to know, and I'm grateful for the opportunity.

As a foster home, I'm given the gift of seeing the dog's potential. But that permanent home is where the dog truly develops under the umbrella of the love and trust. That's where the dogs become who they can be. And that's where the owner uncovers and dusts off that diamond and shines it up.

Happy Tails hopes you will open the umbrella of love and trust in your heart and adopt a rescue.

IN THE END, WE HUMANS
ARE THE LUCKY ONES.
MARK LEVIN, *RESCUING SPRITE*

E-mail Addresses and Web Sites

Did you know that you can search the Internet to find the right dog for you? There's a world full of breeders, rescue groups, and even specific breed rescue associations with Web sites to explore without being emotionally involved. That's what my husband and I did. As a result, we adopted the two best dogs we've had in forty years of dog ownership, and our next dog will be a rescue too.

If you want to rescue a specific breed, go to the American Kennel Club's Web site for a list of contacts: http://www.akc.org/breeds/rescue.cfm. You can also view dogs available for adoption at http://www.petfinder.com (the temporary home of 266,340 adoptable pets from 11,418 adoption groups); http://www.1-800-save-a-pet.com; http://www.pets911.com; and the animal shelters of the American Humane Society.

The Ultimate Rescue

While rescue groups need many people to adopt many dogs, God only needed one person to rescue His people. So He sent His Son—One for all—in the greatest rescue of all time.

God's plan began when He "set eternity in the hearts of men" (Ecclesiastes 3:11 NIV).

Today God draws us with loving kindness; proves His faithfulness over our lifetime; and continually offers His invitation to "Come." To every tribe and nation, He says, "Come."

> *For God so loved the world that He gave*
> *His only begotten Son, that whoever*
> *believes in Him should not perish but have*
> *everlasting life. For God did not send*
> *His Son into the world to condemn*
> *the world, but that the world*
> *through Him might be saved.*
>
> JOHN 3:16–17

If you've reached the point in your life where you feel like you're at the end of the road and need to be rescued, consider these key Scriptures.

Romans 3:23 *For all have sinned and fall short of the glory of God.*

Romans 6:23 *The payment for sin is death. But God gives us the free gift of life forever in Christ Jesus our Lord.* (NCV)

Romans 5:8 *God demonstrates His own love toward us, in that while we were still sinners, Christ died for us.*

Romans 10:13 *For "whoever calls on the name of the LORD shall be saved."*

Romans 10:9–10 *If you declare with your mouth, "Jesus is Lord," and if you believe in your heart that God raised Jesus from the dead, you will be saved. We believe with our hearts, and so we are made right with God. And we declare with our mouths that we believe, and so we are saved.* (NCV)

Romans 12:2 *Do not be shaped by this world; instead be changed within by a new way of thinking. Then you will be able to decide what God wants for you; you will know what is good and pleasing to him and what is perfect.*

Revelation 3:20 *Behold, I stand at the door and knock. If anyone hears My voice and opens the door, I will come in to him and dine with him, and he with Me.*

John 14:19 *Because I live, you also will live.* (NIV)

Therefore, "Do not work for food that spoils, but for food that endures to eternal life, which the Son of Man will give you. On him, God the Father has placed his seal of approval" (John 6:27 NIV). What is the work we are to do? " 'This is the work of God, that you believe in Him whom He sent' " (John 6:29).

Heavenly Father, You promised Your Word would not return void. May everyone who reads these words put their faith in Your Son and be rewarded with eternal life in His Name.

ACKNOWLEDGMENTS

IN MEMORY OF BO:

PRAISE AND THANKFULNESS TO:

God for His faithfulness.
Mac and Bo for the great joy they've given me.

WITH DEEP GRATITUDE TO:

Chattahoochee English Springer Spaniel Club of Greater Atlanta
Zippy Cooper, coordinator
Pete and Martha Dorland, Bo's rescuer.
Christi Cooper, Bo's foster mom.
Lorrie Backer, Mac's rescuer.
Karen Foster, Mac's foster mom.

WITH SPECIAL GRATITUDE TO:

Joyce Hart, Lisa Stilwell, Sandra Malench, and Mark Gilroy.
My faithful prayer partners and sisters.

I welcome your comments at www.LindaWinn.com.